RACING IN
DONCASTER

A Silk-Hatted St. Leger

DONCASTER MORE SMARTLY GARBED THAN GOODWOOD!

Sir Charles Hartopp

Lord Rothschild

Photos

The King arrives at Doncaster

Illustrations Bureau

Doncaster, this year, furnished a sharp contrast to the last great race-meeting in the matter of male attire. While at "Glorious Goodwood," thanks to a hint from His Majesty, the formal "topper" was entirely discarded for a cooler headgear, at Doncaster (a much more democratic meeting than Goodwood) the silk hat was re-instated by the same Royal exemplar, and those who fondly prophesied its disappearance from enclosures may consider themselves snubbed

A page from *The Bystander*, September 1906, featuring Sir Charles Hartopp, Lord Rothschild, and King Edward VII. A caption below the pictures reads, 'Doncaster, this year, furnished a sharp contrast to the last great race meeting in the matter of male attire. While at "Glorious Goodwood", thanks to a hint from His Majesty, the formal "topper" was discarded for a cooler headgear, at Doncaster (a much more democratic meeting than Goodwood) the silk hat was reinstated by the same Royal exemplar, and those who fondly prophesied its disappearance from enclosures may consider themselves snubbed.'

RACING IN DONCASTER

PETER TUFFREY

The History Press

For Cynthia and Jane.
Thanks for all the good times at Doncaster Museum & Art Gallery.

First published 2009

The History Press
The Mill, Brimscombe Port
Stroud, Gloucestershire, GL5 2QG
www.thehistorypress.co.uk

© Peter Tuffrey, 2009

The right of Peter Tuffrey to be identified as
the Author of this work has been asserted in accordance
with the Copyrights, Designs and Patents Act 1988.

British Library Cataloguing in Publication Data.
A catalogue record for this book is available from the British Library.

ISBN 978 0 7524 5342 2

Typesetting and origination by The History Press
Printed in Great Britain

CONTENTS

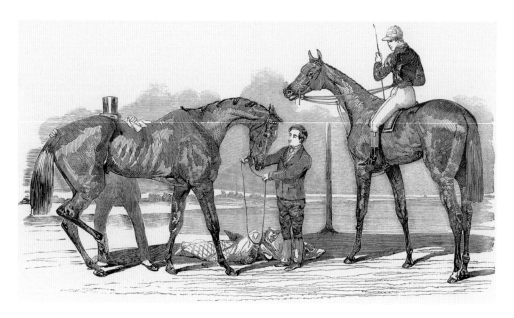

Knight of St George, St Leger winner, 1854.

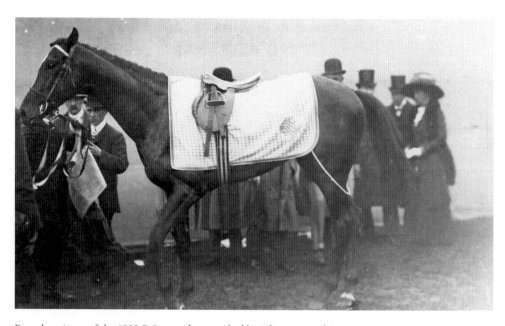

Bayardo, winner of the 1909 St Leger, photographed by Edgar Leonard Scrivens.

INTRODUCTION

I arrived at Doncaster Museum and Art Gallery one dull day in May 1975 to start work as Keeper of Fine and Decorative Arts. I was twenty-one, and for the previous four years I had attended Doncaster College of Art and Leeds College of Art respectively, emerging with a BA (Hons) in Fine Art. While at Leeds, described at the time as the most influential since the Bauhaus, I was part of Jeff Nuttall and John Fox's 'Counter Culture' being crazily involved for the first year with street theatre and happenings.

It was fortunate that I kept my feet on the ground in the following two years, embroiling myself in conventional drawing and print-making under the expert guidance of Wilton Priestner and Norman Webster, as this was to prove useful in the years ahead. My art heroes at college were Edvard Munch, James Ensor and George Grosz, all belonging to a modernistic period of which I prided myself on being fairly knowledgeable.

So, I was disappointed, when I first glanced over the permanent collection at Doncaster as, unfortunately, none of my heroes were represented. The Art Gallery and Museum, as it was known since the year of inception in about 1909, had never employed anyone qualified to curate or display the collection in any erudite fashion. My colleagues in the museum, eccentric individuals to say the least, yet all marvellous experts in their own fields, wished me luck with the task ahead.

The collection mainly consisted of third-rate English artists active between 1780 and 1960, but there were a few pockets of interest. These included a small section of modern British works from the Edward Marsh Collection and a vast amount of paintings and prints depicting scenes from Doncaster's racing history, extending back over 200 years.

Besides being charmed by the horses, all with spindly legs and anxious eyes hurtling towards a finish line or posing proudly after a St Leger or Gold Cup win, I was astounded by their quality. They were mainly aquatints of which I had learned a lot about at Leeds and I was overwhelmed by their masterly execution. These without doubt were my favourite images in the entire collection numbering about 1,000 works.

A friendship of sorts blossomed with the museum curator, Terry Manby, and myself, and in 1976 it was up to the pair of us to stage a massive exhibition for the Bicentenary of the St Leger, pulling in objects and paintings from all around the country. I made a solitary trek up to Dundee to retrieve a Doncaster Cup, followed by Terry and myself journeying in a large van to Newmarket and the hallowed confines of the Jockey Club to raid their collection. It was a fascinating experience to say the least; time had almost stood still in this club festooned with racing objects and paintings.

So, from street theatre in Leeds to the sleepy opulence of the Jockey Club, it really was a cultural leap for me. The St Leger exhibition comprised seventy-four priceless, quality objects and was extremely well received by the general public and brought massive publicity to the efforts of Terry and myself. It really made people aware that the town had a rich racing history.

Thereafter, I developed a deep interest in sporting art but it has taken me thirty-three years to get round to producing something on Doncaster's racing history, being busy in the meantime with a variety of other local history projects, mainly featuring aspects of Doncaster's past.

In this book I have used many reproductions of paintings and prints, and drawn upon my old mate, Edgar Leonard Scrivens, using (as I have done on many occasions in the past) some of his wonderful photos from the Edwardian period. David Appleyard allowed me to reproduce some of his father's fine paintings and watercolour drawings of the St Leger finish and race winners. I am indebted to professional photographers Phil Callaghan and Richard Benson for including some of their unique works; to Stuart Hastings and Jane Smart for allowing access to the unique holdings in the *Sheffield Star*'s library archives.

Compiling this book has been most enjoyable, bringing back fond memories of the time spent at Doncaster Museum and Art Gallery arranging the 1976 Bicentenary St Leger exhibition. I hope it brings similar pleasure to all.

1

AROUND THE RACECOURSE

The betting ring, sketched from the Grand Stand used in the *Illustrated London News* of 26 September 1846.

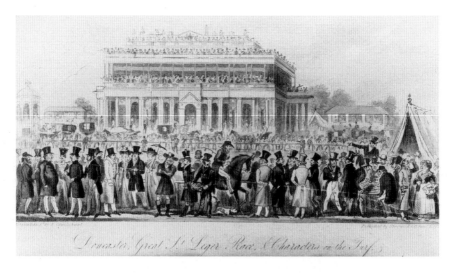

Isaac Robert Cruikshank (1789–1856) engraved this drawing for *The English Spy: An Original Work, Characteristic, Satirical, and Humorous. Comprising Scenes and Sketches in Every Rank of Society, being Portraits of the Illustrious, Eminent, Eccentric and Notorious*, published in two volumes, twenty-four parts in all, in 1825 and 1826. The text was by 'Bernard Blackmantle', a pseudonym for Charles Molloy Westmacott, with illustrations drawn and engraved by Robert Cruikshank. This drawing (part XXII, opp. p. 312) shows 'Doncaster, Great St Leger Race, & Characters on the Turf' and illustrates 'A Familiar Epistle to Bernard Blackmantle, Esq., being a Humorous Description of Doncaster Races, the Great St Leger, Horses and Characters, in 1825. By a Honest Reviewer'. In the list of plates (p. xiii) there is an added sub-title, 'Well-known Heroes of the Turf, Legs and Loungers'.

'A Day out at Doncaster Races' from the *Illustrated London News* of 1850. According to J.S. Fletcher, in his book *The History of the St Leger Stakes 1776–1901* (1902), 'Horse racing...was in favour at Doncaster in the sixteenth century. That there was a race-course on the Town Moor at the very beginning of the seventeenth century is proved by an order made by the [Doncaster] Corporation. It is dated 2 May, 1600, and provides, "That whereas Hugh Wyrrall, gentleman, hath caused a stoope to be sett on Doncaster More at the west end of the horse-race, yt Mr Maior, Mr Huscroft, and Mr Levett maye likewise sett a workman to cutt down or dig upp the sayd stoope."'

[ANNOUNCING THE WINNER OF THE ST. LEGER.]

Announcing the winner of the St Leger, an illustration from *The London Journal; the Weekly Record of Literature, Science and Art* (published from 1845 to 1906). A British penny fiction weekly, it was one of the best-selling magazines of the nineteenth century. The St Leger is four years older than the Derby, which was founded in 1780.

Portrait of Doncaster Race Committee in about 1890. From left to right, the members are: 'Anelay (Borough Steward), Councillor Baddiley, Councillor Stacey, Robert Brooks (assistant Town Clerk), Councillor Dowson, Councillor Pawson, Councillor Brightmore, R. Stockill (Chariman), Councillor Abbott, Alderman Wainwright, Councillor Windle and Councillor Birkinshaw.

'Weighing the Jockeys at Doncaster Racecourse', from the *Illustrated London News* of 18 September 1875, where the following was stated, 'When it came to the preparations for the decisive contest, there were certain arrangements to be observed with which every habitual frequenter of such meetings is probably familiar; the ordeal of "weighing the jockeys" is one prescribed by rule and reason, upon the most obvious considerations.' The Jockey Club laid down the rules for horse racing and created offices to carry out the rules. For instance, the Clerk of Scales weighed out jockeys prior to every race and checked that correct weight, colours and number were carried. After the race, he again weighed in jockeys to ensure correct weight had been carried.

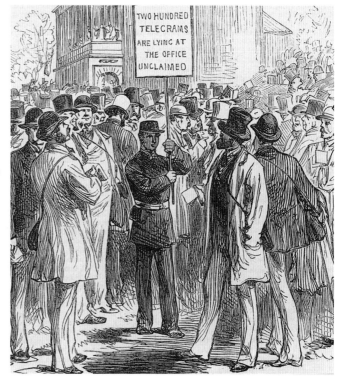

'Doncaster Races: 200 telegrams unclaimed' from the *Illustrated London News* of 18 September 1875. The magazine stated, 'The telegraph office on the Doncaster-course has been enlarged for this year's meeting, but the amount of work that has been imposed on it was beyond all preceding example. A great number of telegrams addressed to persons on the course lie in the office unclaimed during several hours of the day...'

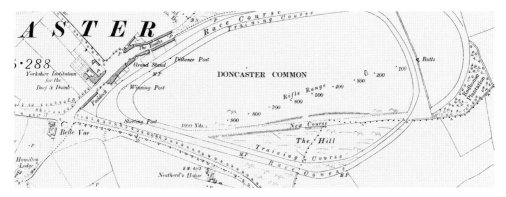

A map of 1904 showing the stands and layout of the course. An interesting description of the course is provided in Benjamin Silliman's *Journal of Travels* (1805–06), 'Near Doncaster I observed the extensive race grounds for one of the favourite amusements of the English. In this instance, an elliptical space, two miles in circumference, was enclosed by a fence; the horses run around this space on a fine green sward, and are kept from flying off, by an exterior railing. Contiguous to the ground there is also a large building which serves as a kind of office or stand for the gamblers of the turf, who are very numerous in Yorkshire. But, racing is fashionable, all over England, and is even encouraged by parliamentary and royal countenance, for the alleged purpose of improving the breed of horses.'

'The race for the St Leger, the scene on the course before the start', drawn by Charles Green R.I. This illustration was featuted in *The Graphic*, 10 September 1892. During the eighteenth century there were a good many alterations in the times and conditions of racing in Doncaster. John Orton, in his *Turf Annals of York and Doncaster* (York, 1844), first mentions race meetings at Doncaster in 1728, when plates of twenty and forty guineas each were run for on 22 and 23 July. 'The meeting of 1729 was held in August, of 1730 in May, and of 1731 in June when it was resolved that June should be the recognised month. By the middle of the century, however, September appears to have been definitely fixed upon as the most agreeable season of the year for celebrating what has since become regarded as an annual event of great importance. There were five days' racing at the September meetings of 1757 and 1758 and four in the following year. After that the races were sometimes on three, sometimes on four days. However, in 1768, sport was particularly poor, there being only a race and a match on the Monday, and the race for the Doncaster Cup on the Wednesday; racing on Tuesday and Thursday there was none, for the good and sufficient reason that there were no horses.'

The scene at the racecourse captured by local photographer Luke Bagshaw. During the nineteenth century, Doncaster was literally besieged and occupied for days before and days after the September meeting, and there was such variety and colour in the High Street and the Market Place, to say nothing of the many strange sights to be seen on the way to the Town Moor and on the course itself. Folk of high and low degree came from far and near, driving in their chariots and their po' chays, mounted on stagecoaches or tramping humbly on foot to take up their residence in the town until the last winner of the meeting had caught the judge's eye, and often for some days later. Inns and houses were filled to overflowing, all manner of sports and pastimes helped to amuse the anxious searchers after pleasure and excitement. There were plays at the theatre and assemblies and concerts in other places of public resort. There were cock pits everywhere and those who admired the noble art could see as much boxing as they cared for. In short, the September week at Doncaster was the great social event of the year, something to be looked forward to.

In the reserved enclosure, Doncaster Racecourse, photograph by Edgar Leonard Scrivens (1883–1950). The gentleman on the left is thought to be Prince Arthur of Connaught. The race meetings on the Town Moor (racecourse) were, in their early days, chiefly patronised by north-country sportsmen. Thus there was a certain strongly local element in the first race meetings – they were the saturnalia of the surrounding district rather than the whole country. In a very curious race-list of the Doncaster race-meeting of 1756, there is abundant evidence that the local magnates were the chief supporters of the event, among the subscribers and names being those of the Marquess of Granby, the Marquess of Rockingham, the Earl of Scarborough, Lord Byron, Sir George Saville, and many representatives of well known Yorkshire and north-country families. There was, indeed, a certain amount of rivalry between the racing fraternities of the North and those of the South, which was never broken down until penny postage had arrived, until telegrams had superseded pigeon expresses, and fast railway trains had brought Epsom and Newmarket next door to Doncaster and York.

The crowd view looking east, photographed by Edgar Leonard Scrivens.

'In the Saddling Paddock', a photograph by Edgar Leonard Scrivens.

'Tick-Tack' men signalling at Doncaster Races. Tic-tac (also tick-tack and non-hyphenated variants) is a traditional method of signs used by bookmakers to communicate the odds of certain horses. It is still used in on-course betting in the UK. A tic-tac man will usually wear bright white gloves to allow their hand movements to be easily seen. A few simple examples of signals: Odds of 9/4 ('top of the head'), both hands touching the top of the head; Odds of 10/1 ('cockle' or 'net'), fists together with the right-hand thumb protruding upwards, to resemble the number 10; Odds of 33/1 ('double carpet'), arms crossed, hands flat against the chest. Essentially, the bookies use tic-tac as a way of communicating between their staff and ensuring their odds are not vastly different from their competitors – an advantage the punters could otherwise exploit. In particular, if a very large bet is placed with one bookmaker, this may be signalled to the others as a way of lowering the price on all the boards.

'In the Reserved Enclosure', a photograph by Edgar Leonard Scrivens.

'Bookies', featuring Tom Boyd of Glasgow. A bookie, bookmaker, turf accountant, or professional better, is someone who analyses, determines, or simply posts the betting odds in games (especially horse racing and team sports). They receive and record wagers from a number of people on a regular basis, collecting from losers, and paying off winners. Bookmaking started in about 1780 at Richard Tattersall's horse auction business. In fact, his name is immortalised at English racetracks today by bookmakers who set up their stands at the 'Tattersall Enclosure.' The term 'bookie' originated with the activity of 'making a book' or keeping a notebook of wagers. In the early days, bookmakers were involved in handicapping. However, chaos prevailed both at the track and in betting shops throughout London until the tradition of the 'honest bookmaker'. A bookie's reputation of honesty was and is very important for the success of the business, and apparently originated with the reputations of two famous bookmakers, Fred Swindell and Leviathan Davies. In about 1850, Davis also created 'lists of odds' that were posted throughout London, which made off-track betting possible.

Racecourse of the Year, 1975. The fifth annual award of the Racegoers' Club was made to Doncaster in recognition of the efforts made by the Racecourse Executive and staff on behalf of the racing public. Doncaster Metropolitan Borough Council's Race Committee Chairman, Albert Cammidge, is pictured second right with Don Cox, the racecourse manager, first right. Information on the Racegoers' Club website states, 'With the Racegoers Club's membership comprising almost 6,000 of the sport's keenest supporters who go racing on average thirty-one times per year, the awards come direct from racecourses' core customer base and therefore hold real importance among British racecourses.'

Scene at the start of the Flat Race Season at Doncaster with Bookies at work on 23 March 1995. In the early 1960s the laws on gambling were relaxed and betting shops on the high street were made legal. Before that time, the only place that most people could have a bet was on the course at the races.

More history was made at Doncaster on 27 July 1992 when it staged the first ever Sunday meeting on a British racecourse. A crowd of 23,000 turned up, despite there being no betting. Father Donal Bambury is seen here on that day leading prayers and attracting the nation's press photographers. *(Reproduced by courtesy of Yorkshire Post Newspapers)*

2

BUILDINGS

Demolition of the Grandstand, 2006. *(Photograph by Richard Benson)*

The Grand Stand was built by a Mr Theakston and Mr Beardshaw from the designs by John Carr of York, at a cost of £2,637, and a minute of the Corporation, dated 2 March 1781, gives order that John Carr shall be paid the apparently very modest sum of one hundred guineas 'for his trouble in architecting and directing' the work. The enterprise of the corporate body did not stop there, however; a new course was formed, the Tryer's stand and the rubbing stables were built, and altogether £7,282 11 7s were laid out for the benefit of the patrons of Doncaster races.

Picture of the Grand Stand, Doncaster, engraved by Rogers. In 1803 Doncaster Corporation decided to make certain alterations with respect to the meeting, by giving an additional day's sport, enlarging and improving the stand, and affecting some other innovations, all of which were carried out in 1804/5. Eric Braim in his article 'Doncaster Architects No 3: William Lindley', published in the *Doncaster Civic Trust Newsletter* of November 1981, says, 'The new work [was] designed by [William] Lindley…The introduction of Ionic Pillars instead of arches at each end which communicated with the wings lately added gives to the room an elegant and light appearance. The building extends in front upwards of 120 ft. the works included a new stewards stand in an octagonal form.' The course was widened and thrown further back from the stand, and there was racing on Monday, Tuesday, Wednesday, and Thursday. The charge for admission to the stand was at this time raised to a guinea. In the *Doncaster Civic Trust News* of September 1990, Eric Braim adds, 'The increasing popularity of the races necessitated a further addition to the Grandstand in 1824.'

The race of 1825 was the fiftieth since its establishment, and the fact probably influenced the stewards in carrying out certain measures which were deemed necessary to improvement. J.S. Fletcher's *The History of the St Leger Stakes, 1776–1901* states, 'A second stand, to be known as the Nobleman's Stand was erected during the year by a subscription of 30 guineas from sixty shareholders among whose names were those of the Dukes of Portland, Cleveland, Leeds, and Devonshire, the Marquieses of Londonderry, Queensbury, Titchfield, and Westminster; Earls Wilton [and] Fitzwilliam.' The actual building amounted to £1,300 and non members were permitted to enter if they were introduced by a member and paid a guinea. On a map of 1841 the stand is noted as the Subscription Stand. Looking at deposited plans in the Doncaster Archives Department it would appear that this stand after undergoing alterations became joined with the Ladies Stand. In the exhibition catalogue *Racing at Doncaster* published in 1976 to mark the Bicentenary of the St Leger Stakes there is listed: 'Ladies Stand Tickets, issued in 1859 when the new Ladies Stand was completed.' The *Doncaster Chronicle* of 1 September 1882 mentioned, 'The stands known as the 'Ladies' and 'Nobleman's' have been undergoing some extensive alterations…'

Local photographer Luke Bagshaw's front view of the Grand Stand where it is plain to see the building has undergone much alteration since its inception. The *Doncaster Chronicle* of 25 March 1937 noted, 'on the stone façade can be read the commemorative inscription: This building finished 1778, Sol. Holmes, Esqr., Mayor.'

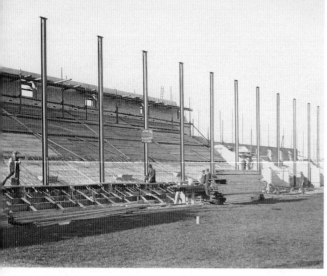

Certain developments at the racecourse towards the end of the nineteenth century and beginning of the twentieth century were recorded by Bagshaw as seen here. It is thought this picture shows work taking place on one of the enclosure stands. The building of the third enclosure stand was competed in 1897. It took place when Alderman Brightmore was Chairman of the Race Committee. A caption on the photograph reads, 'New race stands showing centering and reinforcement in place ready to receive concrete.' A fourth enclosure was erected in 1909 when Alderman J. Pawson was the Chairman.

Another view taken by Luke Bagshaw looking east.

One of the terraced enclosure stands, looking west, photograph taken by Luke Bagshaw.

A view of the stands looking east by an unknown photographer. Within this complex were the following: Astley's Stand, County Stand, Reeds' Stand, Ladies and Nobleman's Stands.

'[The Lincoln or] the Second Enclosure Stand, with the clock on the roof, was built in 1881, when Alderman Stockil was chairman of the Race Committee,' reported the *Doncaster Chronicle* of 25 March 1937. It also added, 'It was extended in 1901.' The stand is still in existence today.

Redevelopments at the racecourse photographed by Luke Bagshaw.

The race stands looking west, photographed by Luke Bagshaw.

The entrance to the Royal Box, which was at the rear of the Grand Stand.

An aerial view of the course at Doncaster taken on 8 September 1936. H.R. Wormald in *Modern Doncaster: The Progress and Development of the Borough from 1836 to 1973–4* (1973) states: 'Over the years the Corporation had built a range of stands which existed in 1965 with the exception of the Ladies Stand built by private subscription in 1859. Post-war improvements were made to the Grand Stand with other amenities and Silver ring on the inside of the course opposite the grandstand was constructed. A contract for the rebuilding of the Grand Stand, due to begin after the Leger Meeting of 1939, was never started because of war restrictions on building and the contract was cancelled under the Defence Regulations.' *(Reproduced by courtesy of Yorkshire Post Newspapers)*

The group of stands pictured from the course before demolition in about 1968. Racecourse manager Noel Nettleship stated in the *Sheffield Morning Telegraph* of 4 February 1970, 'The [new] stand was badly needed. For a racecourse which ranks along with Ascot, Epsom, Goodwood, York and Sandown, the stand area was a hotchpotch.' In the same newspaper Race Committee Chairman John Staniland mentioned, '[The old Grandstand] had been altered and added to so often over the years that it no longer possessed any real architectural merit.'

A general view of the area where a new stand was to be erected at Doncaster racecourse. The picture shows, in particular, the footings and workings being prepared. Wormald states, 'The Totalisator was introduced for betting purposes under the Racecourse Betting Act, 1928, and the Totalisator Board gave grants for approved improvements to the course but the Horserace Levy Board formed under the Betting Levy Act in 1961 took over these functions and was later responsible for the greater part of the money for the building of the New Stand built on the sites of the various stands.' *(Photograph reproduced by courtesy of Sheffield Newspapers)*

The view from the course showing the new stand nearing completion during 1969. The building won an award for the record time in which it was erected. One of the main features of the new stand was the internal betting hall, thus allowing of the transference of the bookmakers from their customary area in front of the stands. This facilitated the Parade Ring to be sited in front of the Grand Stand and a view of the horses parading was in sight to all racegoers in all the enclosures. The Betting Hall occupied two and a half acres of floor area.

Lord Halifax opens the new stand which was built from pre-cast concrete sections.

Opposite, bottom: The new stand under construction during the early 1990s; Richard Budge's construction company helped with the building work.

The new stand was well angled to the course and protection from the weather was provided by a 78ft cantilevered concrete roof and by armour-plate glass screens at each end of the balconies. The *Sheffield Morning Telegraph* of 4 February 1970 said, 'The new St Leger stand, paid for by a grant and loan from the Horserace Betterment Levy Board and funds provided from reserve and borrowing by the race committee, has already seen 12,000 people under its shadow at one time. From it they have seen and will see a standard of racing that has long put Doncaster in the international racing bracket.' The building had a relatively short life span, being recently demolished and replaced by a new structure.

Demolition of the stand that was only thirty-seven years old. This photograph was taken on 27 April 2006 by Richard Benson.

Following an extensive £34.5 million redevelopment, Doncaster Racecourse was officially reopened by HRH the Princess Royal on 12 September 2007 for the four-day St Leger Festival. The development involved the replacement of the old Stand with the state-of-the-art Urban-i Stand and Lazarus Exhibition Hall, providing quality facilities to racegoers and exhibition and conference attendees. Other improvements include the refurbishment of the St Leger Stand, the construction of a new stable block and stable lads' hostel adjacent to the racecourse, the conversion of the old weighing room into the new Champagne and Seafood Restaurant and a new pre-parade ring and saddling boxes. *(Photograph by Richard Benson)*

3

GLASGOW PADDOCKS

Glasgow Paddocks, Waterdale.

Sketches from the *Illustrated London News* of 1885 showing Tattersall's sales on Glasgow Paddocks, Waterdale.

A view of Glasgow Paddocks facing north. Eric Braim in his 'Doncaster Streets – No. 3 Waterdale' published in the *Doncaster Civic Trust News* September 1989 no. 58, mentions that the Waterdale Closes were leased to Lord Clifden for his racing stud, stud groom William Cunningham, and from 1860 they were leased to Lord Glasgow and were known as Lord Glasgow's Paddocks for nearly a century. He also adds, 'Edward Somerset had the Paddocks at the end of the nineteenth century and the [Doncaster] Corporation took them on lease in 1902. The blood stock sales were held opposite the Salutation until the field was developed for the Regent Square houses. In 1860 the sales were held in the Horse Fair [Waterdale] and in 1866 they were moved to Lord Glasgow's Paddocks. A description of the sales in the Horse Market at Race Week in 1862 said they would be worth a journey in themselves. The circle of bidders and spectators comprised all that was distinguished in the sporting world and many who were great elsewhere.'

Glasgow Paddocks facing north. On 7 August 1908 the *Doncaster Chronicle* reported that, 'The most important matter discussed by the [Doncaster Corporation] Council [in Committee] was the proposed purchase of Glasgow Paddocks. A sub-committee had been in negotiation with the tenant for life, Mr A. Browne, and they recommended that the property be purchased for the sum of £24,000. This recommendation the Council adopted, with practical unanimity. The property included not only the paddocks themselves comprising about 14 acres of land, but two houses at the corner facing Christ Church Schools. We understand that the purchase price will be paid out of revenue, and that the paddocks will continue to be used for Tattersall's yearling sales and will also be opened for recreational purposes.'

Leading horses on to Glasgow Paddocks, Waterdale, Doncaster. From 1866 to 1957, blood stock sales on the Glasgow Paddocks in Waterdale, Doncaster, were an annual feature in the town during September. Tattersall's lease ran out in 1957 and they chose not to renew it and concentrated their efforts in the south of England with the result that there were no sales in Doncaster for a period of five years. This was felt to be very detrimental to the town and local businesses and in the early 1960s Albert Cammidge, the DMBC Race Committee Chairman, approached Willie Stephenson and asked him to consider restarting sales using part of the racecourse stables at Belle Vue. At the time, Willie Stephenson was the only Englishman to train both Derby and Grand National winners. He joined forces with Kenneth Oliver, a well known Scottish-based auctioneer and National Hunt trainer, and they started the existing Doncaster Bloodstock Sales in May 1962 and reintroduced the St Leger Yearling Sales in 1963 while a full programme of sales dates throughout the year were gradually implemented. Since then, DBS has grown from a small regional company which specialised in servicing the needs of the commercial marketplace in Britain to its present-day standing as a leading international bloodstock auctioneer with a worldwide reputation of offering value for money and a personal service that is second to none to their clients.

A 1951 aerial view looking from the west across Glasgow Paddocks. This picture gives some idea of the extent of the paddocks. Waterdale is in the top left hand corner.

4

JOCKEYS

Fred Archer.

Archer, Frederick James, was born in Cheltenham on 11 January 1857, the son of William Archer (winner of the Grand National on Little Charlie in 1858). He was the most successful sportsman in horse racing during the Victorian era. The National Horseracing Museum describes him as 'the best all-round jockey that the Turf has ever seen.' Not until the arrival of Steve Donoghue and Sir Gordon Richards were his statistics threatened. Archer was Champion Jockey for thirteen consecutive years until 1886, riding 2,748 winners from 8,084 starts including twenty-one Classics. In 1885 he rode 246 winners, a record that wasn't broken until Gordon Richards' 1933 season. He won the Epsom Derby five times and won a total of twenty-one Classic races. However, because of his height (5ft 10in) he had to diet far more than other jockeys. This had an effect on his health, and after suffering from depression following the death of his wife, Helen Rose, Fred committed suicide by shooting himself on 8 November 1886. The National Horseracing Museum displays a selection of Archer memorabilia, including the gun with which he shot himself during a fit of delirium. He won the St Leger Stakes in 1877 on Silvio; 1878 on Jannette; 1881 on Iroquois; 1882 on Dutch Oven; 1885 on Melton; and in 1886 on Ormonde.

Buckle, Francis (1766–1832), born in Newmarket, started racing at the stables of Richard Vernan, making his first appearance in 1783 at the age of seventeen. His first win in one of the English Classics came in 1800, when he won both the St Leger Stakes and the Epsom Derby on Champion. In his career, Buckle rode twenty-seven Classic wins, including five Derby winners, nine Epsom Oaks and two St Leger stakes (in 1800 on Champion and in 1804 on Sancho). He principally rode for Lord Grosvenor, but also rode for Sir Charles Bunbury, Colonel Mellish, and for the Grafton stable. He continued riding until 1828, aged sixty-five.

Cannon, Herbert Mornington (1873–1962) was born on 21 May 1873, on the day that his father Tom Cannon rode the colt Mornington to victory at Bath. As well as the name, Cannon Snr also passed on his winning ways, 'Morny' being only thirteen when he rode his first winner, becoming a leading jockey and Champion six times. He won the St Leger twice: in 1894 on Throstle; 1899 on Flying Fox and the Doncaster Cup on Winkfield's Pride in 1897. Cannon's great nephew is Lester Piggott.

Carson, William 'Willie' Fisher Hunter, OBE was born in 1942 in Stirling, Scotland. He was British Champion Jockey five times (1972, 1973, 1978, 1980 and 1983), won seventeen British Classic races, and passed 100 winners in a season twenty-three times for a total of 3,828 wins, making him the fourth most successful jockey in Great Britain. In 1983, Willie Carson was made a Member of the Order of the British Empire for his services to horse racing. He is almost certainly the only jockey in the twentieth century to have ridden a horse that he bred, Minster Son, to victory in one of the Classic races, the St Leger Stakes in 1988. Five feet tall and riding at an easily maintained weight of 7st 10lb, he was much in demand as a jockey up to his retirement in 1996 at the age of fifty-four. He has won the St Leger three times: in 1977 on Dunfermline; 1983 on Sun Princess; 1988 on Minster Son, and the Doncaster Gold Cup in 1986 on Longboat and 1989 on Weld.
(Photograph by Phil Callaghan)

Challoner, Thomas, was born at Manchester in 1839. As a boy he worked at the Ashgill stables under John Osborne and won his first race at Liverpool in 1855 on Mr Buckley's Sister. His first year's racing resulted in sixteen wins out of fifty-three mounts. In 1861, on Caller Ou, he obtained a remarkable victory in the St Leger over Luke Snowden on Kettledrum, the odds against the mare being 100 to 1. He notched up five St Leger wins: in 1861 on Caller Ou; 1862 on The Marquis; 1867 on Achievement; 1868 on Formosa and in 1875 on Craig Millar.

Childs, Joe (1884–1958) was born in Chantilly, France's racing headquarters, and rode his first winner at Lincoln at the age of sixteen. Spells riding in France followed, then in Germany, where he began his association with trainer Frederick Darling. At the start of the First World War he returned to England, but during the hostilities he had regular leave from the 4th Hussars to race, and in return in 1918 gave all his riding fees to regimental funds – including those for Gainsborough's Triple Crown glory. He became first jockey to King George V in 1925, riding for him and his trainer, William Rose Jarvis, for ten years. It was said that Childs 'was a great exponent of winning races with a well-timed rush.' In all, he achieved four St Leger wins: in 1918 on Gainsborough; 1921 on Polemarch; 1925 on Solario and in 1926 on Coronach. In 1921 he also won the Champagne Stakes at Doncaster on Golden Corn.

Dettori, Frankie, leaps from his mount Shantou after beating the field to win the 1996 St Leger. Lanfranco 'Frankie' Dettori MBE was born in 1970 in Milan, the son of Sardinian jockey Gianfranco Dettori, who was a prolific winner in Italy. In 1990, Frankie became the first teenager since Lester Piggott to ride 100 winners in one season. On 29 December 2000 he received an honorary MBE. He is well-known for his distinctive 'flying dismounts'. He has won the St Leger five times; in 1995 on Classic Cliché; 1996 on Shantou; 2005 on Scorpion; 2006 on Sixties Icon and in 2008 on Conduit. His successes in the Gold Cup include: in 1994 on Arcadian Heights; 1996 on Double Trigger and in 2006 on Sergeant Cecil. *(Photograph by Phil Callaghan)*

Donoghue, Stephen (1884–1945). In the 1920s the familiar shout on the racecourse was 'Come on Steve' as British punters urged on their sporting idol. Born in Warrington, Steve Donoghue had his initial rides in France and Ireland. He returned to England with a retainer from Henry Persse's Stockbridge Stable in 1911, and in 1913 he rode The Tetrarch for him. By the end of 1914 he had become Champion Jockey for the first of ten consecutive occasions. Donoghue always rode with dash and courage and had magical hands. However, best of all he really loved the horses. 'I think of them as my friends, my greatest friends,' he said. Donoghue won the St Leger twice: in 1915 on Pommern and in 1917 on Gay Crusader as well as the Champagne Stakes in 1913 on The Tetrach.

Jackson, John, was trained by John Mangle and, riding for six different owners, he won the St Leger eight times: in 1791 on Young Traveller; 1794 on Benningbrough; 1796 on Ambrosio; 1798 on Symmetry; 1805 on Staveley; 1813 on Altisidora; 1815 on Filho da Puta and in 1822 on Theodore. About the last winner, Fletcher recalls, 'The circumstances attending Theordore's starting at all were indeed almost farcical. Bets of the most extravagant kind were made – one person laid 1,000 guineas to a crown piece against him, another £1,000 to a walking stick…To add to the ludicrous quality of the affair, John Jackson, on receiving his order to ride Mr Petre's colt, actually burst into tears, and exclaimed, "What! Ride such a cripple as that?" However, he did ride him, and faithfully stuck to his orders…striking his spurs into the animal's flanks as soon as the flag fell and getting away with a clear lead which he never lost, ultimately winning by four lengths…'

Piggott, Lester Keith, born 5 November 1935, is famously tall for a jockey (5ft 8in), hence his nickname of 'The Long Fellow'. He is considered to be the best of his generation and the greatest flat jockey of all time, with 4,493 career wins, including eight St Leger victories: in 1960 on St Paddy; 1961 on Aurelius; 1967 on Ribocco; 1968 on Ribero; 1970 on Nijinsky; 1971 on Athens Wood; 1972 on Boucher and in 1984 on Commanche Run. Piggott won his first race in 1948, at twelve years old, on a horse called The Chase at Haydock Park and became a teenage sensation. He rode his first winner of the Epsom Derby in 1954, when he was just eighteen. He pioneered a new style of race-riding that was subsequently widely adopted by colleagues at home and abroad and enabled him to become Champion Jockey eleven times. There can be little doubt that, had he not chosen after the 1971 season to ride more selectively, he would have won more championships. *(Photograph by Phil Callaghan)*

Richards, Gordon. He was born in Shropshire in 1904, the son of a miner and one of twelve children. It was said that 'with his unorthodox style, long reins, upright and slightly twisted torso' he rode in a class of his own, and was Champion Jockey on many occasions, becoming Sir Gordon in 1953. He rode five St Leger winners: in 1930 on Singapore; 1937 on Chulmleigh; 1940 on Turkhan; 1942 on Sun Chariot and in 1944 on Tehran. He also won the Champagne Stakes at Doncaster in 1932. He died in 1986.

Scott, William, was born at Chippenham in 1793, and was introduced to the saddle at a very early age, riding continually from 1814 to 1847, his last mount being his own horse Christopher in the Derby of that year. Tykes and northerners believed that 'Glorious Bill' would go on winning as long as he liked to throw his leg across a horse. From 1838 to 1841 he had a monopoly of the St Leger, riding nine winners: in 1821 on Jack Spigot; 1825 on Memnon; 1828 on The Colonel; 1829 on Rowton; 1838 on Don John; 1839 on Charles XII; 1840 and 1841 on Launcelot and in 1846 on Sir Tatton Sykes. He died at Highfield House, near Malton, in 1848, full of honours gained during a busy and brilliant career.

Singleton, John, rode Alabaculia the first winner of the St Leger, for the 2nd Marquess of Rockingham, in 1776. He was born on 24 June 1732; his father was a horse dealer. John became a jockey at the age of sixteen, and rode first at Kirkby Lonsdale. Singleton's last ride was at Chester in 1784. At one time he had raised sufficient money to purchase a horse, which broke its leg in running at Barnswood. Leaving the turf, he commenced business as a horse dealer, and afterwards as horse-breaker and farrier. He was ninety-four when he died.

Watts, John (1861–1902), was born at Stockbridge, Hampshire, became an apprentice to Tom Cannon, and rode his first winner at the age of fifteen in 1880. On joining trainer Richard Marsh, he worked his way up to be stable jockey. It was said that 'Watts was a natural horseman with a quiet effective style.' He retired to train at Newmarket in 1900, dying two years later. He won the St Leger five times: in 1883 on Ossian; 1884 on The Lambkin; 1890 on Memoir; 1892 on La Fleche and in 1896 on Persimmon. His last winner was for H.R.H. the Prince of Wales.

Weston, Tommy (1903–81), was born in Dewsbury, Yorkshire, the son of a railway wagon driver. He became apprenticed to E. McCormack, a Middleham trainer, at the age of fourteen, when he weighed 4st 3lbs. Later, the trainer recommended Weston as stable jockey for Lord Derby, a post he held for ten years, winning eight Classics for his patron. The relationship lasted until 1934. Weston won many more races including three St Legers: in 1923 on Tranquil; 1928 on Fairway and in 1933 on Hyperion. He was described as a dashing jockey, with very sympathetic hands, being popular with everyone. He was Champion Jockey in 1926.

Wootton, Frank (1894–1940), was known as a boy wonder, riding his first winner at Turffontein in South Africa at the age of nine, and his first in England when he was thirteen. He won his first Classic in 1909, and the St Leger, on Swynford owned by the 17th Earl of Derby, a year later. During the First World War, he served with the Army in Mesopotamia and later took out a licence to train, recording over 100 winners. He returned to Australia in 1933, dying in Sydney seven years later. He always argued that Swynford was the best horse he ever rode.

5

ON THE RACECOURSE

Parade for the 1912 St Leger. *(Photograph by Edgar Leonard Scrivens)*

A sweepstake of 25 Guineas was held over two miles on Cantley Common, two miles east of the current Doncaster racecourse, on 24 September 1776. The rules stipulated that colts should carry 8st of weight, and fillies 7st 12lb. The event was organised by Charles Watson-Wentworth, 2nd Marquess of Rockingham (a prominent politician and former Prime Minister) and was the idea of Lieutenant Colonel Anthony St Leger (a former MP). On the day, the winning horse (from a field of five) was owned by Rockingham, with a horse owned by St Leger following in second. The event didn't receive its name until a meeting held between the 1777 and 1778 meets. When it was suggested that the race should be called the Rockingham Stakes, the Marquess is said to have replied: 'No it was my friend St Leger who suggested the thing to me – call it after him.' In 1779, the race moved from Cantley to a new course on the Town Moor, where it remains to this day. The race for the St Leger of 1812, illustrated here, was won by Otterington. The picture is a painting by Clifton Thompson titled 'Panoramic View of British Horse Racing'.

The start of the 1830 St Leger, a print by Smart and Hunt from the painting by James Pollard (1797–1859). The race was won by Birmingham. Earlier, in 1809, in consequence, according to W. Sheardown's notes, of 'the increasing celebrity of these races' were erected the buildings which later became the home of the Deaf and Dumb children. The buildings (on the left here) were originally intended for use as an additional stand and stables, and built as a private speculation by a Mr Maw. However, the venture appears to have been quickly diverted from its first purpose. It was subsequently used as an educational establishment for young ladies, under the guidance of Miss Murphy, and afterwards as a school for boys, conducted by Dr Inchbald, and, in 1830, it was sold to the Yorkshire Deaf and Dumb Institution.

'Approbation – Off in Good Style,' for the St Leger of 1836, painted by James Pollard, engraved by J. Harris. During the mid-nineteenth century there was opposition to Doncaster Corporation's contributions to the races both in the council and in the town generally, but in 1860 the corporation was wholly responsible for the September races and the maintenance of the course. The Spring meeting, first held for one day in March 1849, was run by a separate management committee over the corporation's course with their permission but in 1863 the management committee gave up the meeting, transferred its funds to the corporation and the Spring meeting became part of the council's racing programme which up to 1939 was of only six days in the year.

'The Race for the Great St Leger Stakes of 1836' depicted in a painting titled 'Anticipation – Who is the Winner?' by James Pollard, engraved by J. Harris. The race was won by Elis. Wormald informs, '[By 1838] racing was generally falling into disfavour … and in 1841 Lord George Bentinck threatened to remove the patronage of the racing confederation elsewhere unless the [Doncaster] Corporation would put up £1,000 for the races and they were compelled to do this for 1842.' The Jockey Club were taking a greater control of racing generally and we find the *Doncaster Gazette* in 1849 remarking that 'the entire management is now confided to the Jockey Club.' Gradually the corporation had to undertake more and more of the expenditure on the course and buildings to keep them fit for racing; the corporation regularly took the advice of the Jockey Club on various matters and by 1869 they were contributing £2,000 yearly in prize money.

James Pollard's 'Joy and Desperation – All Over But Settling', part of a series of four paintings depicting events from the 1836 St Leger. All of these were engraved by J. Harris. The series included Plate 1: 'Vexation – the False Start'; Plate 2: 'Approbation – Off in Good Style'; Plate 3: 'Anticipation – Who is the Winner?' and Plate 4: 'Joy and Desperation – All Over But Settling'. For the first thirty years of the nineteenth century, the St Leger was the most successful of the race meetings.

The 1838 Doncaster Gold Cup Of 1838 painted by J.F. Herring (1795–1865). The race was won by Don John, owned by Lord Chesterfield. The horse also won the St Leger in the same year. Around the mid-nineteenth century, a National Hunt Committee ran its meetings independent of the council, using the Low Pastures and the course for the purpose. The *Doncaster Chronicle* for 8 March, 1849, gave a plan of the hunt course but in 1894 they gave up using the Low Pastures and used the Common and the Stands for their steeplechases. At this time, the round course was in its present position but the straight mile alongside Sandall Beat Road was not constructed until 1910.

The dead heat for the Doncaster Great St Leger Stakes between Charles XII and Euclid, 1839, an engraving by Charles Hunt after a painting by John Frederick Herring. The thoroughbreds were both three-year-olds, foaled in 1836.

The decisive heat for the Great St Leger Stakes at Doncaster, from a painting by J.F. Herring, engraved by Chas Hunt. In the run-off, Charles XII just won by a head. He was afterwards sold for 3,000 guineas, but later for only £50, the lowest price at which the winner of a selling handicap could be offered, and even then the purchaser forfeited his deposit of £20 rather than take him.

In *The History of the St Leger Stakes, 1776–1901*, Fletcher mentioned that 'punctually at three o'clock [at the September race meeting of 1874] the thirteen numbers of the starters were hoisted on the telegraph board, and the jockeys at once proceeded to the paddock, where the competitors were already saddled. Very little time was wasted in mounting and before five past three the whole of the mounted competitors began to file their way on to the course. The course, which as usual was admirably kept, was cleared nearly to the Red House – fully half a mile from the winning-post; and the competitors at once proceeded to go through their preliminary canters. They got to the post in capital time, and at the first attempt a false start was made, all getting off in good order with the exception of Boulet. After returning, they were again marshalled into line by Mr M'George and at 3.28 an excellent start was effected.'

'Start for the Great Yorkshire Handicap on 6 September 1910', by Edgar Leonard Scrivens. The *Doncaster Chronicle* of 3 June 1910 reported that, 'The Race Committee of Doncaster Corporation are determined that the famous Town Moor shall not suffer by comparison with other courses and [a] scheme of improvement has now commenced. The chief of these…is the making of the new straight mile. It will be two years, probably, before this will be fit for use…Before the making of the new course could be entered upon the Corporation had to acquire 27 acres of land from Earl Fitzwilliam, and 3 other acres from the Red House Farm…The new course was staked out last week and the timber is now being cleared off the land through which the new track will be made. It is expected that two years will elapse before the turf is fit for thoroughbreds to race upon. When completed it will be a very fine improvement, providing spectators with a view of mile races, and making it possible for the last five furlongs of any race to be on a straight course.'

'At the Starting Gate', photographed by Edgar Leonard Scrivens in about 1912. Scriven was a renowned local topographical photographer who took many Doncaster race views.

'A Good Start', photographed by Scrivens.

'Parade for the St Leger' showing the eventual winner, Night Hawk, trained by W.T. Robinson at Foxhall, photographed by Edgar Leonard Scrivens. The *Doncaster Gazette* of 12 September 1913 recalled the race highlights: 'The parade in order of the card took place very punctually, and the white flag was hoisted only one minute after the advertised time. At the first attempt three or four of them were through the tapes and there were about a couple more failures before Mr Willoughby effected an admirable start… [At one time in the race] Night Hawk [was] a long way last but eventually closed rapidly on the leaders… [In time] White Magic assumed the command from Seremond at the distance, but was challenged by Night Hawk a hundred yards from home, the latter winning by a couple of lengths.'

'A St Leger Parade' by Edgar Leonard Scrivens. In 1927, a radio commentary was made for the first time from the Doncaster course by the BBC.

A racecourse scene photographed in about 1930 by local photographer, Edgar Leonard Scrivens.

'In the Saddling Paddock' by Edgar Leonard Scrivens. Racing at Doncaster was interrupted by the two world wars, the course being requisitioned by the military authorities. Between 1915 and 1918 the St Leger was run at Newmarket. After the outbreak of the Second World War on 3 September 1939, the race for that year was cancelled. From 1940 to 1945 the race was staged at Thirsk, Manchester, Newmarket and York.

The parade for the St Leger from a painting by Joseph Appleyard (1908–60), a prolific artist in watercolours and oils of landscape and sporting subjects from the mid-1930s until his untimely death in 1960. After the Second World War the Doncaster race track was slightly altered to give a one-mile spur into Sandall Beat Wood and when the corporation began their National Hunt meetings the track for this purpose was laid out inside the round course. The number of days' racing increased from the pre-war six days to twenty-one days in 1971, with racing under both Jockey Club and National Hunt rules and mixed flat and jumping races at certain of the meetings. The *Doncaster Gazette* of 19 September 1959 stated, 'Although total attendances for the four day meeting did not reach those of last year, Saturday's figures were stated to be slightly up. This despite fears expressed by Ald. A.E. Cammidge, Chairman of Doncaster Race Committee that the charity meeting at Sandown would draw racegoers away. It was the first time that another meeting had competed with Doncaster St Leger Day.'

The finish of the 1959 St Leger, painted by Joseph Appleyard. The race was won by Cantelo, ridden by Eddie Hide and owned by William Hill. The value to the winner was £28,636 5s. The *Doncaster Gazette* of 19 September 1959 informed, 'On the day of the big race a pall of smoke threatened to obscure part of the course. It came from Red House Farm, where in the early hours fire had destroyed £2,000 worth of barley, corn and straw and menaced the stables of Doncaster trainer Mr Eddie Magner. Smoke from the smouldering debris could be seen throughout the day. As colourful as ever were the race-going crowds and the feminine fashions. Eighty planes made use of Doncaster Airport during the meeting.'

Moment of triumph, the photographers are waiting for Nijinsky and Lester Piggot as they return to the winner's enclosure after a convincing St Leger victory in September 1970.

A dead heat in the race between Ballybunnion, the favourite (E. Mercer) and Don Rickardo, a 100-8 outsider, with Double Light third; Ballybunnion is no. 9. (*Reproduced by courtesy of Sheffield Newspapers*)

Horses parading before one of the races in September, 1980. (*Reproduced by courtesy of Sheffield Newspapers*)

Right: Willie Carson pictured at Doncaster races during the 1980s. *(Photograph by Phil Callaghan)*

Below: The Cammidge Trophy Finish, 26 March 1983, with Lester Piggott bursting through to win on Vorvados from Famous Star and Camiste. The Cammidge Trophy, a listed race for talented sprinters over six furlongs, is named in honour of a former chairman of Doncaster Racecourse and Mayor of Doncaster, the late Albert Cammidge OBE. *(Reproduced by courtesy of Sheffield Newspapers)*

A picture dating from 22 March 1984 on the opening of the flat season at Doncaster. Spanish Place ridden by Steve Cauthen is seen beating Golden Flute USA (no. 9) with John Lowe up. Third is Tetron Bay with Lester Piggott up (in quartered cap). *(Reproduced by courtesy of Sheffield Newspapers)*

The William Hill Lincoln Handicap finish at Doncaster on 28 March 1987. The winner, Star of Gunner (J. Reid up on left in striped shirt), beating the field at the post. The William Hill Lincoln Handicap — a famous Heritage Handicap over the straight mile which traditionally begins the new flat season — was first held at Doncaster in 1965. *(Reproduced by courtesy of Sheffield Newspapers)*

'Love You Rosy', ridden by Philip Barnard, wins the South Yorkshire Training School Handicap at Doncaster on 26 June 1987. The South Yorkshire Training School Apprentice handicap was the race designed to focus attention on jockeys of the future. *(Reproduced by courtesy of Sheffield Newspapers)*

Presentation at the Medical & General Ltd Handicap Trial race at Doncaster Racecourse during 2007. *(Photograph by Richard Benson)*

Race action at Doncaster during 2007. *(Photograph by Richard Benson)*

Race to the finish line; action at Doncaster during 2007 in front of the new stand. *(Photograph by Richard Benson)*

6

OUTSIDE THE RACECOURSE

Tram and race traffic. This view of a race-day crowd at the Hall Gate/High Street junction was taken
in about 1902 from dentist Thomas Cuttriss's first-floor balcony window.

The Subscription Betting Rooms were erected at a time when Doncaster races were probably the most fashionable in the north. The *Doncaster Gazette* of 25 August 1826 declared that, 'These splendid rooms from the designs of Woodhead and Hurst are nearly finished.' The same newspaper of 11 May 1950 stated that, 'In their palmy days the rooms were the resort of the elite of the racing fraternity and the club membership was considerably over a thousand. The rooms were known throughout the country and were considered to have played a great part in making Doncaster racing meetings popular…Up to 1871 the club would seem to have a remarkably successful run. In this year however detectives from Bradford raided the premises and the raid seems to have resulted in considerably lessening the rooms' popularity. The final blow to this enterprise came a short time later when by-laws were passed prohibiting such places for the purpose of betting.'

The scene outside Doncaster railway station during race week from the *Illustrated London News* of September 1875.

The *Illustrated London News* of 15 September 1849 had two interesting pictures, one captioned 'The Rail – The Horse Box' and the other 'The Road – The Horse Van', and a small piece about how the arrival of the railway into Doncaster had affected the races. 'The railway has, at length, reached this sporting metropolis of the north; and, if we have lost the pastime of posting down to Doncaster to witness the Leger run for, we have gained what would really astonish the old school as much as did the facts of Eclipse-viz. the wonder of leaving London on the morning of the St Leger, seeing the great race decided, and returning to the metropolis the same day…On Monday afternoon the trains from Leeds, York and Manchester brought a small increase of visitors; but it was not until the arrival of the special train by the Great Northern line that the slightest approximation to the bustle which might reasonably have been expected on the eve of a great meeting was observable. Nine-tenths of the metropolitan turfites adopted this route; and it is due to the directors and their officials to state that, although the line into Doncaster has only opened one week, there was not the slightest confusion; the hours of departure and arrival were punctually observed, and the passengers, one and all expressed their unqualified satisfaction with their trip.'

Salutation Inn, South Parade, Doncaster. The *Doncaster Gazette* of 11 September 1908 stated that, 'The "public house" which in the early part of the eighteenth century marked the building hunt of the town in that direction was named "The Salutation" in 1782. "It was" says the *"Doncaster Gazette"* historian of 1868 "associated for years with the huge fame of Messrs Tattersall." [The horses that] were stabled at this inn [included]: The Colonel (St Leger 1828), Touchstone (St Leger 1834), The Baron (St Leger 1815), Newminster (St Leger 1851), West Australian (Two Thousand Guineas, Derby and St Leger 1853).' Eric Braim in his 'Doncaster Streets – No. 3 Waterdale' from the *Doncaster Civic Trust News* September 1989 no. 58 mentions, 'The blood stock sales were held opposite the Salutation until the field was developed for the Regent Square houses. In 1860 the sales were held in the Horse Fair [Waterdale] and in 1866 they were moved to Lord Glasgow's Paddocks.'

A day out at Doncaster races showing the road to the course, a print from the *Illustrated London News* of 1850. By the middle of the nineteenth century the St Leger, like the Derby, had become a great popular institution. The rapid development of the railway system was every year making it more and more possible for the masses to join in what in the old days had been almost exclusively the sport of the upper classes, and Doncaster began to witness an annual invasion of people from here, there and everywhere. Lord William Lennox in his *Pictures of Sporting Life and Character* published in 1860 stated, 'The high-mettled racer no longer plods his weary way over the hard, dusty road, but is conveyed to the scene of action in a four horse van, on the railway track; and sportsmen are conveyed from London to Doncaster for the small sum of ten shillings on Ledger and Cup days.'

'Doncaster Races Sweepstake Lunch Romance' a painting by E. Brentnall reproduced in the *Illustrated London News* of 1890.

A good many associations of the old days of racing at Doncaster centred around the theatre in the Market Place. It was built in the year which saw the foundation of the race for the St Leger stakes. The St Leger was first run on 24 September 1776, and the new theatre was opened on the preceding evening, all previous theatrical performances up to then having been given in the Guild Hall. This new departure owed a good deal to General St Leger, by whose interest, joined to that of Mayor Rickard and several other gentlemen of the town, and Mr Tate Wilkinson, lessee of several other theatres, was enabled to build it in 1775–76. The following passage from his memoirs gives an interesting sidelight on Doncaster races in 1776, 'I closed Wakefield Theatre on Saturday September 21, and opened the new theatre at Doncaster on Monday, September 23, 1776… and a very pretty, elegant theatre it then was and now is. Of course the novelty of the theatre and the numerous attendances at the Races made it a fashionable place of resort.' Wilkinson himself was a clever actor, and knew how to keep a good company together, and, until his death in 1803, he seems to have taken pains to provide sportsmen who turned to his theatre after an afternoon's racing with good entertainment.

THE ILLUSTRATED
LONDON NEWS

REGISTERED AT THE GENERAL POST-OFFICE FOR TRANSMISSION ABROAD.

No. 2527.—VOL. XCI.   SATURDAY, SEPTEMBER 24, 1887.   TWO WHOLE SHEETS | SIXPENCE. BY POST, 6½D.

News announcing the Hexthorpe rail crash on the front cover of the *Illustrated London News* of 24 September 1887.

The Hexthorpe rail accident occurred on 16 September 1887 at Hexthorpe railway platform, some 1½ miles west of Doncaster on the line to Sheffield and Barnsley. The platform was situated within a block section between Hexthorpe Junction and Cherry Tree Lane and so had no signals of its own. The railway platform was a simple wooden structure on the Doncaster-bound line, usually used for the collection of tickets from the many trains arriving in the town for the St Leger race meeting. The usual method of working the 1½-mile section of line was to pass trains from Hexthorpe Junction under a 'permissive' block ruling, not usually used on passenger lines, with additional control by two flagmen spaced between the junction box and the ticket platform. On that day two trains were in the section, the first, a Midland Railway train, stood at the platform, the second, another Midland train, waiting just to its rear. As the first train moved off, the second moved onto the platform so that tickets could be checked. The third train in this scenario was a Liverpool to Hull express worked by a MS&LR crew. This train came over Hexthorpe Junction with, first the 'distant' signal and then the 'home' signal at danger. With speed down to a crawl, the 'home' signal was lowered, the driver assumed, wrongly, that with no other fixed signals to Cherry Tree Lane his route was clear and speed gradually rose. In the official report it was said that the first of the flagmen gave no indication and the second gave an ambiguous signal which was seen by the fireman but not properly understood. The express was reported doing between 35 and 40mph when they rounded the curve and saw the Midland train still on the platform. The driver applied the 'simple' vacuum brake and threw the locomotive into reverse but could not stop with the short distance of less than 250 yards. In total, twenty-five people were killed and sixty-six injured.

Rick Johnson, holding the reins on his wagonette, was a horse and general dealer at Mexborough near Doncaster, and just one of the many individuals who adapted their businesses to cater for the needs of those wanting to attend Doncaster races. Rick is pictured in about 1907 with passengers outside the South Yorkshire Hotel, Mexborough, before travelling to the races.

The rear of Belle Vue House, now the Grand St Leger Hotel. The property was built in about 1811 on an area of land called Haigh's Close, for John Henry Maw, by Alderman Lockwood. Originally it was to be titled the Turf Hotel and was to include training stables; however, it became John Henry Maw's house. For much of the twentieth century the house was used to accommodate stable hands. On 9 September 1937 the *Doncaster Gazette* commented, 'Do you know of the best view of the famous 'straight mile' on the Doncaster Racecourse is to be had? It is scarcely likely that you do and you cannot buy a ticket for the privilege of watching the races from this vantage point. One man has, for seventeen years, [acquired] almost the sole rights of it. He is Mr Jack Lindsay, who since 1920 has been caretaker at Belle Vue House, which will be a temporary home for some five hundred stable boys…' The *Doncaster Civic Trust Newsletter* of July 1980 reported that the DMBC had decided to offer Belle Vue House for sale, the race committee having provided new accommodation for the stable lads. Also, as the council had no further use for the house, it was proposed to apply to the DoE for permission to demolish it. However, the house was acquired by local builder J. Gamble who opened the premises as the Grand St Leger Hotel in 1984. Sometime afterwards the building was damaged by fire and in 1990 was taken over by the Din family, who made additions to the premises.

The Rockingham Inn, Bennetthorpe, Doncaster, built in 1778, is named after the horse of the same name which won the 1833 St Leger. The inn is situated on a main thoroughfare to the racecourse. A few public houses in Doncaster and the surrounding areas took their names from the town's association with horses and horse racing; the Turf Tavern, the Horse and Jockey, Horse and Groom, Rockingham, Tararre (formerly at Tickhill but now defunct), and St Leger Tavern. The vast influx of visitors to Doncaster during the race meetings in the early days transformed the town into a vast lodging place. However, Wormald reflected in 1974 how racing's effect on the town had changed, 'The influx of people in Leger week still fills the hotels but the motor car and its speedy transport to and from the course no longer makes it necessary for private parties to hire houses for the week and so pay householders' rates for the year as was supposed to happen pre-1939. The Races bring no profit to the rates and apart from some employment probably do not bring much in the way of cash to the town.'

The scene here, according to a caption beneath the image, 'depicts an auction sale of stalls and spaces outside Doncaster racecourse. W.H. Dewhurst, the auctioneer, who had conducted the sale for a number of years, is seen standing in the wagonette.'

Race traffic pictured adjacent to Doncaster railway station, 13 September 1911. The rapid building up of the railway system revolutionised race-meetings altogether as far as attendances were concerned and everything underwent a change. At Doncaster the altered aspect of affairs seems to have met with speedy recognition. New stands, giving accommodation to racegoers and to people whose business brought them to the races, were erected on the Town Moor; the surroundings of the Grand St Leger were much improved; the telegraph wires were brought to the very theatre of events, and superseded pigeons which had formerly been the swiftest messengers human thought could devise, and provisions of all sorts were made for making the place the scene of a great annual event.

Race Booths, on Grand Stand Road, provide refreshments for racegoers in the 1930s.

Crowds leaving the racecourse. It was reported in the *Doncaster Gazette* of 14 September 1933 that the great trek to Doncaster races, 'began over the weekend. Saturday saw the arrival of the first of the caravanners, who pitched their camps on the Town Moor and elsewhere. In late years caravans have been resplendent affairs drawn by motor cars, and among the campers this year were many holidaymakers enjoying to the full life in new and picturesque surroundings.'

An aerial view looking towards Grand St Leger Hotel. 'With most of the pits in the district on holiday large numbers of miners tramped into the town,' said the *Doncaster Gazette* of 14 September 1993. It also added, 'Times are hard at many of the pits and there is nothing like the amount of money they had to spend a few years ago. In many cases miners were up by dawn and walked into the town to save train and bus fares. Hundreds were also early abroad to watch the gallops.'

Two views from the Great North Road, Doncaster, looking towards the Grand Stand, by Edgar Leonard Scrivens. At the 1934 St Leger, the BBC added a little realism to their account of the St Leger by including in their news bulletin on the day of the race a 'sound impression in which there was heard road traffic noises, engine whistles, the arrival of an aeroplane, snatches of fairground music, tipsters' cries, bookies shouting their prices in the ring, and finally a short commentary on the actual Leger race.'

7

RACE CUPS
AND OTHER ITEMS

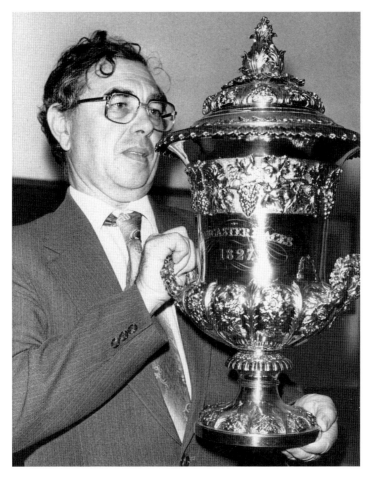

The Doncaster Gold Cup of 1827 pictured with former Doncaster Museum
curator Terry Manby. *(Reproduced by courtesy of Sheffield Newspapers)*

Gold or silver racing cups of elaborate form were given as prizes in the biggest horse races. Their designs became increasingly sculptural and naturalistic. They often depicted events in British history or episodes in historical novels that were linked to the locality of the racecourse. The 1784 Gold Cup was won in 1784 by Phenomenon, owned by Sir John Lister-Kaye, of Denby Grange near Wakefield. It is a silver-gilt two-handled cup with cover and the artists were Andrew Fogelberg and Stephen Gilbert (active 1781–95). *(Reproduced by courtesy of Sheffield Newspapers)*

The silver Doncaster Cup of 1817 resembles a campana vase – an inverted bell shape, stylishly popular at the time and intended to be used as a wine cooler. *(Reproduced by courtesy of Sheffield Newspapers)*

A silver-gilt cup by Rebecca Emes (active 1808 until about 1829). The cup is engraved on one side: 'Doncaster Races 1827', on the other: 'His Grace the Duke of Devonshire, the Most Noble the Marquis of Titchfield, Stewards.' In 1827 the cup was won by Earl Fitzwilliam's jockey, S. Day.

The taste for replicas or adaptations of famous antique vases was characteristic of British Regency silver, and Piranesi's plates provided the designs for such metalwork. The silversmiths Rebecca Emes and Edward Barnard created this Doncaster Cup in 1828, a reduced version of the Buckingham Vase. Rebecca Emes is presumed to be the widow of John Emes (partner to Henry Chawner). She registered its first hallmark with Edward Barnard in 1808 and was active until about 1829. The firm was undoubtedly one of the largest working in the Regency Period and had wide connections in the trade. They were suppliers of plates to the Royal Goldsmiths, Rundell, Bridge and Rundell (the same firm that retailed Paul Storr's silver), to Cattle and Barber in York with race cups and were firm favourites with the English community in India who only bought top quality silver of good gauge.

Left: Picture from the *Illustrated London News* of 18 September 1847, the newspaper having the following to say, 'The Doncaster Cup… is a vase, in the mixed *cinque-cento* and Arabesque style. The base and stem are richly chased, and the bowl has bold bosses, scroll-work, and moulding, of superb character. The cover bears an excellently modelled group from the best age of chivalry – an incident in the battle of Ascalon, in which Richard I unhorses a Saracen warrior, and repels the attack of a spearman who assails him on foot. The Monarch wears the ringed armour and the cylindrical helmet, of his time, and the other combatants are in the Saracenic costume. A palm tree overshadows the group, and improves its pyramidal effect, while it characterises the locality of the heroic incident…It has been modelled by Mr Cotterill, and is a very spirited and elegant composition. The work is in silver, dead and burnished, admirably executed, at the establishment of Messrs Garrard, of the Haymarket, to whom the order for it was given by the Stewards of the race-Lord Strathmore and Sir John Gerard Bart.'

Below: The Doncaster Cup of 1845, won by Sweetmeat, is a silver centrepiece for a large dining table. It shows an ancient Greek hero riding his four-horse chariot at the Olympic Games. *(Photograph reproduced by courtesy of Sheffield Newspapers)*

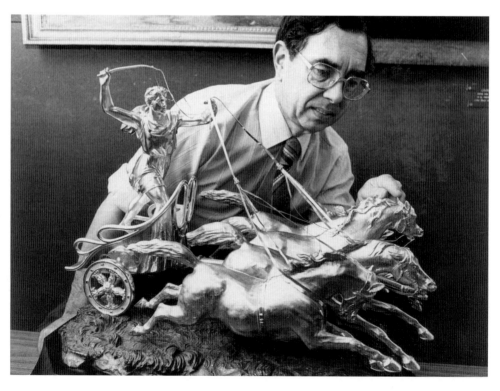

Above left: The Doncaster Cup of 1849, picture from the *Illustrated London News* of September 1849.

Above right: Illustrated London News of 21 September 1850 had this caption beneath the illustration, 'This superb prize cup, run for at Doncaster on Friday, has been manufactured at the establishment of Messrs Hunt and Roskell (successors to Storr and Mortimer) of Bond Street, from a model by Mr Alfred Brown. It consists of an elegant cup, of the Cinque Cento style of ornament. On the cover are two groups of horses – wild and domesticated – surmounted by a figure of Victory crowning a horse with a wreath. On the bowl of the cup are four compartments filled with designs in low relief, representing four different styles of racing – the English, the Italian, the ancient Roman, and a race by torchlight. Around the foot of the cup is cleverly grouped horse furniture. The pedestal is of ebony, and bears the names of the Stewards of the Races, and 'Doncaster, 1850' inscribed in Silver. The height of the whole is between three and four feet, and the value upwards of 300 guineas. It is altogether a magnificent plate.'

The Doncaster Race Cup of 1853 is silver and in the form of a centrepiece showing the captive King John of France entering London on May 1357, escorted by the Black Prince to whom he had fallen captive at the Battle of Poitiers. The cup was won by Lord Rothschild's horse, Hungerford, and designed by Baron Carlo Marochetti (1805–67/68) being made by C.F. Hancock of London. The cup's ownership passed from the Baron Meyer de Rothschild by descent to the 6th Earl of Rosebery and sold at Sotheby's Mentmore sale, May 1977. The *Illustrated London News* of 17 September 1853 informs, 'The subject, was we understand, suggested to the artist by Lord Ribblesdale, whose good taste and zeal for the sports of the turf are well known.' *(Reproduced by courtesy of Sheffield Newspapers)*

Right: Design for the 1854 Doncaster race cup in ink wash by sculptor Henry Hugh Armstead (1828–1905). This drawing is typical of the designs for silver that were produced in the 1850s. It illustrates a scene from Sir Walter Scott's novel *Ivanhoe* (1819), set in the Yorkshire forest of Jervaulx Abbey (not that far from the Doncaster racecourse). The episode shows the Prior of Jervaulx restraining a Norman knight from striking the impertinent Saxons.

Below: From the *Illustrated London News* of 17 September 1864 where the following comments were made, 'The Doncaster Cup…is from the establishment of Messrs R. and S. Garrard and Co. of the Haymarket. The design consists of a group of figures representing a hawking party in the time of the Cavaliers. The principal figure is a lady, who is on horseback; in the foreground is an attendant who has the charge of two dogs, and by the side of the lady is another attendant holding the hawk.'

The Doncaster Shield in silver parcel-gilt by J.S. Hunt. This is the cup for 1865 and was won by Ackworth, owned by the 4th Marquess of Hastings. Only one or two were made in the form of a shield. The circular relief in the centre depicts the meeting of Bolingbroke and the Earls of Westmorland and Northumberland at Doncaster in 1339. Previous owners have included the 4th Marquess of Hastings and the Worshipful Company of Fishmongers. It was sold at Christie's in January 1979. *(Reproduced by courtesy of Sheffield Newspapers)*

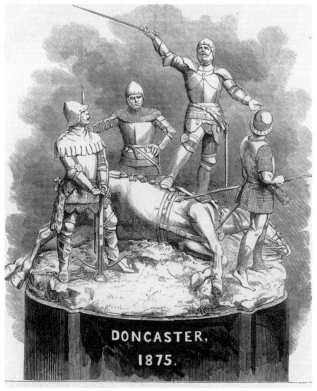

The following information under the heading 'The Doncaster Cup' was printed alongside the picture reproduced in the *Illustrated London News* of September 1875. 'This piece of plate was manufactured by Messrs Hunt and Roskell, of New Bond Street. Its design [was] modelled by Mr G. A. Carter… The subject of the group is taken from Hume's account of the battle of Towton Field AD 1460. We read that, previous to the commencement of the action, the Earl of Warwick, finding that the numbers of the Yorkists (on whose side he fought at the time) were inferior to those of the Lancastrians, endeavoured to raise the spirit of his army by slaying his own horse, and declaring his intention to fight on foot like a common soldier. The result of the battle was a complete defeat of the Lancastrian forces.'

Right: St Leger Centenary mug. *(Reproduced by courtesy of Sheffield Newspapers)*

Below: Silver Burgess Ticket. One of the tickets issued to holders of Burgage property in Doncaster as compensation for their loss of grazing rights on the race common. It is oval, with the arms of Doncaster Borough, and inscribed, 'Doncaster Corporation: Race Common. No. 8. Date May 1894. This token is the property of the owner ---- Doncaster.' Inscribed on the reverse: 'This token entitles the owner to tickets for the grandstand and saddling paddock at race meetings under the control of Corporation on the conditions confirmed.' *(Reproduced by courtesy of Sheffield Newspapers)*

YR.	WINNER	JOCKEY	Sub.	Running Time
1801	QUIZ	SHEPHERD	11	8	
1802	ORVILLE	J SINCLETON	15	7	
1803	REMEMBRANCER	R. SMITH	23	8	
1805	SANCHO	BUCKLE	24	11	
1806	STAVELEY	JACKSON	27	10	
1807	FLYDENER	CARR	39	15	
1808	PAULINA	CLIFT	41	16	
1809	PETRONIUS	SMITH	28	12	
1810	ASHTON	SMITH	51	14	
1811	OCTAVIAN	CLIFT	40	8	3.30
1812	SOOTHSAYER	SMITH	63	24	
1813	OTTERINGTON	JOHNSON	57	24	3.31
1814	ALTISHOORA	JACKSON	50	17	
1815	WILLIAM	SHEPHERD	53	12	
1816	FILHODAPUTA	JACKSON	59	15	
1817	DUCHESS	SMITH	16	13	
1818	EBOR	JOHNSON	52	18	
1819	REVELLER	JOHNSON	51	21	3.15
1820	ANTONIO	NICHOLSON	50	14	3.48
1821	ST.PATRICK	JOHNSON	72	27	3.24
1822	JACK SPIGOT	SCOTT	49	13	
1823	THEODORE	JACKSON	73	25	3.32
1824	BAREFOOT	CODDISON	84	12	3.23
1825	JERRY	SMITH	77	13	3.29
1826	MEMNON	SCOTT	88	30	3.22
	TARRARE	NE.SON	95	27	3.26

Left: Doncaster Gold Cup. The photograph is dated 1939 on the reverse. There is also the following caption, 'The Doncaster Gold Cup supplied by Messrs H.L. Brown and Son Ltd, 65 Market Place, Sheffield and 17 High Street Doncaster to the order of Doncaster Race Committee. It weighs over 31oz, and is in Elizabethan design. It is a beautiful example of Sheffield craftsmanship.' *(Reproduced by courtesy of Sheffield Newspapers)*

Below: The caption on the reverse of this picture reads, 'Visitors who flocked to Doncaster racecourse to look over the course prepared for Leger week admire the 1956 Doncaster Gold Cup on show in the Royal Box. September 1956.' *(Reproduced by courtesy of Sheffield Newspapers)*

The caption on the reverse of this picture reads, 'Doncaster Coronation Cup 10 September 1953.'
(Reproduced by courtesy of Sheffield Newspapers)

The Doncaster Gold Cup in a photograph dated 7 September 1964 on the reverse.
(Reproduced by courtesy of Sheffield Newspapers)

Left: Labelled on the reverse is the following, 'The Doncaster Gold Cup to be competed for at Doncaster Town Moor next Thursday valued at £500 made of solid gold on a green onyx base with a Filial also of onyx. The cup is almost 18in high, designed by Reginald Hill. The cup is exempt from purchase tax as the design is approved by the design centre.' *(Reproduced by courtesy of Sheffield Newspapers)*

Below: The Chafer Great Yorkshire Handicap Trophy of 1976. *(Reproduced by courtesy of Sheffield Newspapers)*

8

RACING CHARACTERS
– A FEW SKETCHES

Hugh Cecil Lowther, 5th Earl of Lonsdale, KG, GCVO (1857–1944).

Aga Khan III, Sultan Mahomed Shah, (1877–1957)
was the forty-eighth Imam of the Shia Ismaili Muslims,
and one of the founders and the first president of the
All-India Muslim League, serving as President of the
League of Nations from 1937 to 1938. He was an
owner and breeder of thoroughbred racing horses,
including six winners of the St Leger (1924, Salmon
Trout; 1932, Firdaussi; 1935, Bahram; 1940, Turkhan;
1944, Tehran; 1952, Tulyar), and a total of sixteen
winners of British Classic Races. He was British flat
racing Champion Owner thirteen times. In addition
to his English Classic successes, the Aga Khan won two
Ascot Gold Cups, two Prix de l'Arc de Triomphes,
a Grand Prix de Paris and thirteen Irish Classics. His
knowledge combined with wealth enabled him to
found a racing empire which had no equal.

Appleyard, Joseph, was a prolific
artist in watercolours and oils of
landscape and sporting subjects from
the mid-1930s until his untimely
death in 1960. Upon leaving school he
attended local evening classes at Leeds
School of Art gaining a job in window
display and general advertising,
limiting his painting to weekends and
weekday evenings. In time he struck
up a friendship with Leeds artist Jacob
Kramer, a forthright critic, whose
kindness and comments encouraged
Joe. Longing to be able to paint what
pleased him, one August morning, he
gave his notice, collected his cards and
that was that! Jacob recommended he approach the *Yorkshire Post* who gave him space of three columns width
by 6in deep each Saturday in their Weekly Edition. This small contract proved to be his salvation for regular
pay gave him a free hand to draw in black and white any subject. His first assignment – 'Polo on the Stray
at Harrogate' – proved horses would play a big part in his career. Joe was killed when he fell from a bus at
Lawnswood roundabout during 1960. Eric Taylor, principal of Leeds College of Art, made this fitting tribute,
'He developed a name for himself in a comparatively short time for his excellent horse portraits.'

Bentinck, Lord (William) George Frederick Cavendish-Scott (27 February 1802–21 September 1848), better known as simply Lord George Bentinck, was an English Conservative politician and racehorse owner. He was best known (with Benjamin Disraeli) for his role in unseating Sir Robert Peel over the Corn Laws. 'Lord George Bentinck's influence on the Turf and on English racecourses from 1833 – and particularly from 1841–1848 was enormous,' said J.S. Fletcher. He also added, 'In the early days when race horses tramped the highways from one meeting to another (for no one seems to have thought of carrying them until Lord George Bentinck caused to be invented the van which conveyed Elis from Goodwood to Doncaster in 1836); [the first van ever used to convey a race horse from one place to another]'. Lord George had an intimate connection with racing at Doncaster and his stud was, for some time, at the Turf Tavern, Bentinck Street, under the charge of a Mr Bowe. Bentinck was particularly admired in many quarters for his efforts to eliminate fraud in the sport. He is commemorated with a statue in London's Cavendish Square Gardens.

Boscawen, Evelyn 6th Viscount Falmouth (1819–89). J.S. Fletcher stated the following about him, 'No greater contrast between owners – so far, at any rate, as far as betting on their own horses is concerned – could possibly exist than that which was afforded by the example of Viscount Falmouth, who, unlike the Colonel Mellishes, the Lord Bentincks and the Sir Joseph Hawleys, never wagered a penny about racing matters in his life.' From the beginning of his racing career until the end he netted in stakes about £300,000; his greatest year being 1878 when he earned £38,000. He will always be remembered in the history of English Turf as one of the very few men who loved racing for itself alone, who never dreamed of betting on the chances of his horses, and as the straightest owner that ever sent a horse to the post. He won all the Classic races on more than one occasion, many of his horses being ridden by Fred Archer. Lord Falmouth won the St Leger three times, in 1877, 1878 and 1882.

Grosvenor, Hugh Lupus, the 1st Duke of Westminster (1825–99) inherited Eaton Stud and was highly successful as a thoroughbred breeder as well as on the track. A major name in racing, among his most famous horses was the undefeated Triple Crown champion, Ormonde, and a second Triple Crown champion, Flying Fox. He was the only man to have been owner/breeder of two winners of the Triple Crown. The meaning of Triple Crown is thus: For colts, the Two Thousand Guineas, the Derby and the St Leger; for fillies, the One Thousand or Two Thousand Guineas, the Oaks or Derby and the St Leger. A winner of the appropriate three Classic races for three-year-olds is a hero or heroine of the Turf. It is believed that the character 'Colonel Ross' in Sir Arthur Conan Doyle's short story *Silver Blaze* is modelled on Hugh Grosvenor. He had three successes as owner and breeder in the Leger, in 1886 with Ormonde; 1899 with Flying Fox and in 1902 with Sceptre.

Gully, John, was a remarkable character and constantly seen on the Doncaster Town Moor during the reign of George IV. He was born in Somerset in 1785, the son of a butcher and died in 1863 a country gentleman, wealthy and much respected, having in the meantime distinguished himself as a boxer, publican, bookmaker, owner of racehorses, proprietor and manger of collieries, as well as a Member of Parliament. The victory of the Hon. E. Petre's Matilda over John Gully's Mameluke in the 1827 St Leger caused considerable controversy. Mameluke, then owned by Lord Zetland, won the Derby of that year, and was bought by Gully at the Ascot meeting for 4,000 guineas. Gully was so full of confidence about Mameluke that he backed the horse heavily for the St Leger but lost £45,000. However, Gully's gains on the turf were enormous and, apart from the Mameluke episode, the St Leger was particularly profitable for him. He backed Memnon, the 1825 St Leger winner, to an enormous amount. The first was 100-25 that Memnon was placed first and Alderman second for the St Leger; the second, 1000-20 that he placed both horses; the third, 15000-1000 that if the two were first and second, Memnon would be first. Gully lived for many years at Ackworth Park near Pontefract but later moved to Durham where he died in 1863.

Hamilton, Archibald, 9th Duke of Hamilton (1740–1819) was a Scottish peer and politician. In 1768, Hamilton became MP for Lancashire and held the seat until 1772. In 1799, he inherited his half-nephew's titles and was appointed his successor as Lord Lieutenant of Lanarkshire. He was the owner of seven St Leger winners: in 1786 with Paragon; 1787 with Spadille; 1788 with Young Flora; 1792 with Tartar; 1808 with Petronius; 1809 with Ashton and in 1814 with William.

Herring, John Frederick. With the St Leger, the name of John Frederick Herring will always be associated, just as it will always be included with those of Stubbs, Sartorius, Garrard, Gilpin, Wooton, Marshall and in later times of M. Emil Adam, in a list of the men who have really known how to paint the horse. He was born in London to a Dutch father and later moved to Doncaster, arriving there in September 1814, in time to see the Duke of Hamilton's William win the St Leger. He found work as a painter of coach signs and as a whip on the Lincoln and Wakefield coach, later being transferred to other runs. He developed an interest in painting and found patronage with various gentlemen including Mr Stanhope at Cannon Hall, Barnsley, and Mr Hawkesworth of Hickleton Park, Doncaster. Eventually he painted the portraits of winners of the St Leger for thirty-three years, that of Filho da Puta (1815) being the first and of the Derby for eighteen years, and he also produced pictures of some of the closest finishes of his time. Herring resided in Doncaster until 1830, thereafter at Newmarket and London, but the last ten years of his life were spent at Meopham Park in Kent, where he died in 1865.

Lambton, George (1860–1945). After a fall at Sandown Park Racecourse in 1892, Lambton decided to take up training and a year later was appointed trainer to the 16th Earl of Derby at Bedford Lodge stables in Newmarket. Lord Derby died in 1908 and was succeeded by his son, the 17th Earl of Derby. George Lambton's work for the family continued uninterrupted and he trained the winners of ten British Classic races, receiving the accolade of British flat racing Champion Trainer in the 1906, 1911 and 1912 seasons. In 1926 Lambton was replaced by Frank Butters as Lord Derby's trainer but remained as his racing manager and resumed training for the earl in 1931. In 1933 however, he was finally replaced by Colledge Leader. He became a public trainer and remained so until his death in 1945. He had four successes in the St Leger: in 1910 with Swynford; 1919 with Keysoe; 1923 with Tranquil and in 1933 with Hyperion.

Lowther, Hugh Cecil, 5th Earl of Lonsdale, KG, GCVO (1857–1944) was an avid sportsman and *bon vivant* and was known by some as 'England's greatest sporting gentleman. He was the best-known figure on the racecourse after the Prince of Wales. Lowther devoted his enormous wealth, derived from the Cumberland coalmines, to a life of ostentatious pleasure. His fondness of yellow for his many cars and footmen's livery inspired his nickname 'The Yellow Earl'. He donated the original Lonsdale Belts for boxing. He was also associated with the management of Arsenal football club. His Royal Lancer was the 33-1 winner of the St Leger in 1922 and Myrobella, owned by him, won the Champagne Stakes at Doncaster in 1932.

McCririck, John, the British television horse racing pundit, born 1940, is seen at Doncaster on 6 September 1995. He often uses the traditional tic-tac signals as part of his pieces to camera when explaining the odds of the horses for the next race. He was originally a racing journalist with *The Sporting Life* and also wrote for *Grandstand*. He began his career as a television pundit on ITV's horse racing coverage in 1981. During 1984 and 1985, horse racing moved to Channel 4. In 2002, Channel 4 launched its own digital television racing channel, at the races, which was sold to BSkyB in 2003. He is famous for his outspoken opinions; in particular, he has risen to the defence of punters when he thinks they are being given bad value, and is highly critical of jockeys when he doesn't think they have ridden well. He is best known to American racing audiences for his annual appearance on the Breeders' Cup telecast, in which he invariably touts British horses over their American rivals.

Mellish, Henry was a distinguished figure of the turf. He was born at Blyth in 1780 and lived at Blyth Hall, situated between Bawtry and Worksop, not far from Doncaster. At Eton he was famous for his mastery of the Classics and his absolute dislike and contempt for all authority. He left there at seventeen to enter the 18th Light Dragoons and later the 10th Hussars. He started out his turf career in 1801 when his horse Welshman, ridden by Peirse, won a match of 50 guineas at Durham. He was a born gambler and lost his money with as much nonchalance as he won it, losing £40,000 at one stage on the throw of a dice. He won the St Leger with Sancho in 1804, and with Staveley in 1805. It was said the colonel never made a bet of less than £500, and he so infected other sportsmen that the betting on the 1806 St Leger

was unparalleled with over 1 million guineas being laid two months before the race. Colonel Mellish kept a splendid equipage for his arrival at race meets. He arrived 'four white horses in hand' pulling his 'exquisitely painted' barouche, 'with outriders on steeds to match.' All followed by his grooms in crimson livery. At the 1806 St Leger he bet more than he could afford and, suffering heavy losses, subsequently fled to the Peninsula, distinguishing himself as aide-de-camp to Sir Ronald Ferguson. He died in 1817 aged thirty-seven.

Monolulu, Ras Prince Monolulu (1881–1965), real name Peter Carl Mackay, was something of an institution on the British horse racing scene, from the 1920s until the time of his death. He regularly attended the Doncaster St Leger meetings and was particularly noticeable for his brightly coloured clothing. As a tipster, one of his best known phrases was the cry, 'I gotta horse!' which was subsequently the title of his memoirs. During the First World War he was interned in Germany. He rose to prominence after picking out the horse Spion Kop in the 1920 Derby, which came in at the long odds of 100–6, and from which he personally made some £8,000 – a vast amount of money at the time. Although claiming to be a chief of the Falasha tribe of Abyssinia, the reality is that he came from the Caribbean island of St Croix (now part of the US Virgin Islands). He styled himself as a prince after being press-ganged on one occasion, assuming that a prince would be far less likely to be shanghaied. Prince Monolulu would sell his tipping sheets in envelopes at all the important race meetings. He was very funny, and would have the crowds in stitches with his banter – just like a market trader, only with much more style.

Montrose, Caroline Duchess of (1818–94) was a breeder and owner of racehorses who also went under the names of 'Carrie Red' and Mr Manton. Married three times, she was described as a formidable woman obsessed with racing, once rebuking a vicar who prayed for fine weather at harvest time, when one of her horses competing in a Classic wanted soft going. After her second husband's death in 1883, she married twenty-four-year-old Harry Milner, forty-one years her junior. Her horse Seabreeze won the 1888 St Leger.

St Leger, Major-General Anthony (1731/32–86) was a successful soldier, MP for Grimsby, and the founder of the St Leger Stakes horse race. Born into the St Leger family, an Anglo-Irish family of Norman stock, he was educated at Eton College, attended Peterhouse, Cambridge, before embarking on a career in the Army. In 1761, he married a Yorkshire woman, Margaret Wombwell. During the same year he was appointed Lieutenant-Colonel of the 124th Regiment of Foot, but a year later the regiment disbanded, and St Leger took on the Park Hill estate in Firbeck, where he later bred and raced horses. From 1768 to 1774, St Leger sat as MP for Grimsby. Two years after leaving the Commons, and with the assistance of Charles Watson-Wentworth, 2nd Marquess of Rockingham, he established a two-mile race for three-year-old horses, on the Cantley Common in Doncaster. This was to become the St Leger Stakes. St Leger died on 19 April 1786. He was buried in St Anne's Church, Dublin.

Stanley, Edward George Villiers, also known as the 17th Earl of Derby (1865–1948), was a prominent breeder and owner of race horses. In turn, the horses also became most influential in the stud book which has lasted to the present day. The heavily moustached, rotund and genial earl held many offices in public life, including Ambassador to France, MP, Postmaster General, Lord Mayor of Liverpool and Secretary of State for War. He was leading owner seven times and leading breeder on ten occasions. His successes in the St Leger included 1910 with Swynford; 1919 with Keysoe; 1923 with Tranquil; 1928 with Fairway; 1933 with Hyperion and in 1943 with Herringbone.

Stockhill, Alderman, the Chairman of Doncaster Race Committee, photographed in about 1895 by Hudson & Kearns, London. A caption beneath the picture reads, 'No inhabitant of Doncaster will fail to recognise the portrait offered above. The portly form and genial face are familiar to all dwellers in the famous West Riding town, and that worthy gentleman it may be added, must be known, to thousands whose only visit to the place is made once a year, at Leger time. The Chairman of the Race Committee is a member of an old Doncaster family resident there for upwards of a century, his father and ancestors having had long business connections with the town. In Municipal matters he has from an early life taken much interest.'

Wentworth, Charles Watson, 2nd Marquess of Rockingham (1730–82), who twice served as Prime Minister, was the fifth son and eighth child in a family of ten. Brought up at the family home of Wentworth Woodhouse near Rotherham, Yorkshire, he owned Alabaculia, the first winner of the St Leger in 1776. The marquess produced a number of fine horses at his Wentworth Stud, was well known in all sporting circles, and followed the example of his ancestors in his devotion to the breeding of race-horses and in his love of fox-hunting.

9

ROYAL AND OTHER VISITORS

King Edward VII is welcomed at the private entrance to the Royal
Box in the Grand Stand at Doncaster Racecourse by Alderman
Pawson (Chairman of the Race Committee) in 1909.

In 1857, Charles Dickens and Wilkie Collins joined forces for their humorous narrative *The Lazy Tour Of Two Idle Apprentices*, which was originally published in *Household Words*, 3–31 October 1857. Unexpectedly, during their tour of 'out-of-the-way' places, they visited Doncaster in what must have been an afterthought for it was never part of their original intentions to visit the town. However, they arrived during race week and this led to many observations on the characters found in Doncaster during the St Leger week. They took quarters in the Angel Hotel, Dickens describing this in a letter as 'very good, clean and quiet apartments on the second floor. Looking down into the main street, which is full of horse jockeys, bettors, drunkards, and other blackguards from morning to night-loud all night.' Dickens had one great stroke of luck while he was in the town describing it as a 'wonderful paralysing coincidence.' On St Leger day he bought a race card and wrote down three names for the winners of the three chief races. Never had he heard or thought of any of the horses. Strangely, those three races were won one after the other by those three horses.

Right: Bing Crosby. In Malcolm Macfarlane's *Bing Crosby Diary, 1960–69*, the entry for 6/7/8 September 1966 reads, 'At Doncaster in South Yorkshire where they attend the races including the St Leger.'

Below: Manchester United supremo, Sir Alex Ferguson, is engulfed by autograph hunters at Doncaster racecourse on 17 August 2007. Sir Alex was the co-owner of Rock Of Gibraltar, which was beaten at Doncaster in the Champagne Stakes by Dubai Destination on 14 September 2001.

Royalty has visited Doncaster Racecourse on a number of occasions. King Edward VII frequently attended meetings; his grandson King George VI and Queen Elizabeth went there in 1948. Her Majesty Queen Elizabeth II has also made a number of visits. Edward VII is pictured above in South Parade in about 1905 while on his way from Doncaster railway station to the racecourse.

Edward VII pictured conversing with Lord Downe and Mr E.C. Clayton. The *Doncaster Gazette* informed, 'His Majesty was not long in appearing on the balcony and he received the customary hearty greeting from the busy crowd of sportsmen in Tattersall's ring, just below. He was looking the picture of health, bronzed and dressed in a black frock coat and a silk hat, and wore a tie of his racing colours and a tiny orchid in his button hole. The king spent the greater part of the afternoon on the balcony, watching the sport through his field glasses, and chatting with his friends, and did not leave until the runners went out for the last race. Unfortunately, the crowd did not have the privilege of cheering a Royal winner to victory. Two of the King's horses were engaged, but neither of them made any show.'

Princess Mary pictured with Lord and Lady Lonsdale in the saddling paddock at Doncaster Races. The *Doncaster Gazette* of 10 September 1926 said it was expected that the house parties of fashionable visitors to the St Leger meeting of that year would be fewer than the previous year, but many of the best-known families were regarding the Doncaster festival with increasing favour as revealed by the many notable names among the lists of those present in the exclusive stands on the course. Foremost among the aristocratic visitors were Princess Mary and Viscout Lascelles, who were again the guests of Lord Lonsdale in a Doncaster house. The newspaper also added, 'Long before the arrival of Princess Mary and Earl Lascelles late on Monday night a crowd had congregated round the entrance to St Vincent, Doncaster, eagerly awaiting a glimpse of the royal visitor. One woman spectator was seen using a pair of opera glasses.'

S. 18. THE KING IN THE GRAND STAND, DONCASTER, 1909.

Edward VII pictured in the Grand Stand. On Wednesday 12 September 1909 the king arrived early, and the sun was shining brilliantly. Though the king was in a covered Mercedes car line, he was everywhere recognised and a popular form of greeting from the man in the street was 'Good luck to Minoru'; the king's beautiful colt. Around the entrance to the stand there was an immense crowd and the king stood for a second or two on the step smiling and doffing his hat in acknowledgement of the vociferous cheers. The puzzle of the race was why Minoru ran so badly, for, as was remarked, no excuse was deliverable. It was of course a keen disappointment, for there had seemed such good reason to hope for and anticipate the king's success. But, while his majesty lost his place at the head of the list of winning owners, he was, at any rate, easily second. There was practically no cheering at all. Bayardo won in dead silence. This was to be the king's last visit to Doncaster.

Left: H.R.H. Princess Anne, pictured up on Final Alma at Doncaster Racecourse during 1987.
(Photograph by Phil Callaghan)

Below: During a trip to South Yorkshire on Friday 25 March 1994, Queen Elizabeth II visited the Mansion House, Doncaster, and honoured the Mayor (Councillor John Quinn) with her presence at luncheon. In the afternoon the queen attended Doncaster Races and was received at the racecourse by the Chairman of the Racecourse Committee, Councillor Ronald Gillies, seen here. *(Photograph reproduced by courtesy of Sheffield Newspapers)*

10

MELTON VASEY

Doncaster racehorse trainer Melton Vasey (on the left).

Melton Vasey's Belle Vue stables, behind the Grand St Leger Hotel. Frederick Melton Vasey, until his death in 1952, was one of the North's leading racehorse trainers. He was born in 1885 at Woodborough, Nottinghamshire, the night before Melton (Derby winner of that year) won the St Leger – hence his name. He was the son of Joseph Vasey, who began life as a farmer, but changed to training racehorses, most notably at Hambleton, Thirsk. Melton rode in his first race when only ten years old. A couple of years later, he rode his first winner, Spittlefields, at Redcar, in June 1897. However, he soon became too heavy for riding on the flat and turned to helping his father. In April 1902, father and son moved to Doncaster; Joseph Vasey only lived in the town for three years, dying in 1905 aged fifty-three. Melton was respected in racing circles for the way he treated his apprentices, unlike some big stables. Following his father's death, Melton took control of the business, running it from stables at Belle Vue (behind the Grand St Leger Hotel). The horses were trained on the racecourse and also the old aerodrome, now the site of the Dome Leisure Centre.

Horses in the Belle Vue stables. Melton left Doncaster in about 1912 and trained horses in Brazil, returning at the outbreak of the First World War. He served in the Army from 1914 to 1918. After the cessation of hostilities, he started training again in Doncaster. His first really good season was in 1924, when he won forty races.

Melton's son Avril (pictured on the right), born in 1907, followed in his father's footsteps. He started riding under National Hunt rules in 1923, having his first winner at Leicester in February 1924, Son o' Lommond, trained by his father. In 1925, local businessman Herbert Mollekin (pictured centre) became Melton's patron, and in 1926 they won thirty-six races. A year later, Melton built Woodborough House (now the Woodborough Hotel) opposite the racecourse stables. At the time, Belle Vue was on the edge of town. There were no Bessacarr or Cantley housing estates, only farmland. Family accommodation at Woodborough House was on the first two floors, with quarters for apprentices on the top floors.

In 1929, Avril Vasey had a bad experience in the Scottish Grand National. He was riding Hereford Lad which was knocked over at the water by Manito. L.B. Rhodes (who rode Manito) though hurt by the fall, saw Avril lying stunned, face downwards in the water and, but for his timely assistance, Avril might have drowned. The death of Herbert Mollekin was a blow to the stables and the Vaseys had a lean time for a year or two, until they won the 1931 November Handicap, with North Drift on the Manchester Castle Irwell Course. Following this, they operated quite a lucrative business with their horses running all over the north of England. Melton had up to a hundred horses stabled at Belle Vue at any on time.

In 1939, many racing buildings were requisitioned for military purposes. The Belle Vue stables were included, with a large Royal Army Veterinary Corps depot being established there. Melton Vasey closed down his training establishment. But, something of the atmosphere of racing was preserved by a number of well-known jockeys serving at Doncaster in the corps. Melton Vasey died in 1952, just before the start of the flat racing season. On the day of the funeral, Avril had his first race winner.

11

WINNERS

Antonio, winner of the 1819 St Leger.

THE CHAMPAGNE STAKES

The Champagne Stakes is a Group 2 flat horse race for two-year-old thoroughbred colts and geldings run over a distance of 7 furlongs at Doncaster Racecourse during the St Leger meeting in September. Since its first running in 1823, many notable horses have contested the race. Slieve Gallion, seen here, won the race in 1906.

The Champagne Stakes of 1910 was won by Pietri, owned by L. de Rothchild and ridden by D. Maher.

It was reported in the *Doncaster Gazette* of 14 September 1923 that Mumtaz Mahal's presence in the Champagne Stakes made the event 'all the more interesting.' Mumtaz Mahal was the highest-priced animal in the Doncaster sales in the previous September, H.H. the Aga Khan paying 9, 000 [guineas] for the spotted daughter of The Tetrach – Lady Josephine. She won the race 'in a hack canter by three lengths. Possessing a wonderful stride, her time was 1[minute] 15[seconds] which, against the breeze, can be considered most satisfactory. A large company awaited her return to the unsaddling enclosure, and the ease with which she scored in the hands of G. Hulme, for the fifth time in succession, greatly increased her reputation.' The National Sporting Library's Thoroughbred Heritage website says Mumtaz Mahal was 'one of the most important broodmares of the twentieth century.' She was named for empress Mumtaz Mahal, wife of Mughal Empire ruler Shah Jahan (of Taj Mahal fame) and bred by Lady Sykes at her Sledmere Stud in Driffield, East Riding of Yorkshire.

THE DONCASTER GOLD CUP

In 1764 the Corporation Plate was founded and the Doncaster Cup was first run on Cantley Common two years later. It is senior to the St Leger by ten years, and, like most of the races of that time, was run for in heats. Touchstone won the race in 1835 and 1836. Touchstone (1831–61) was a British Thoroughbred racehorse and champion sire. Owned and bred by Robert Grosvenor, 1st Marquess of Wesminster, he was conditioned for racing by the pre-eminent trainer of the day, John Scott. His most important win as a three-year-old came in the 1834 Classic, the St Leger Stakes. He went on to win the Doncaster and Ascot Gold Cups twice, retiring having won fifteen of his twenty starts, including six walk-overs.

Beeswing (1833–54) raced at many venues between 1835 and 1842 and was a real crowd favourite. In her day, Beeswing was hailed as the greatest mare in Britain and one of the greatest of all time. Entering sixty-three events, she won an incredible fifty-one times. Of the fifty-seven races she finished, she was placed lower than second on only one occasion. Beeswing won the Doncaster Gold Cup in 1837, 1840, 1841 and 1842 as well as the Champagne Stakes in 1835. Such was her fame that the Scottish village of Lochend, Dumfries and Galloway, changed its name to Beeswing in her honor.

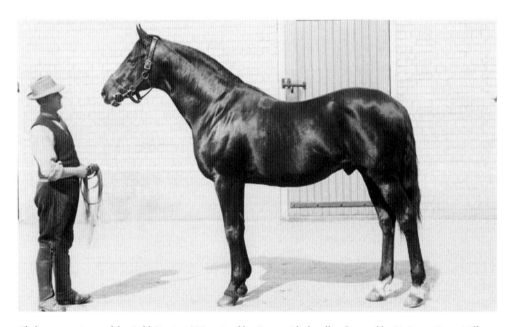

Chaleureux, winner of the Gold Cup in 1898, trained by George Blackwell and owned by Sir James Percy Miller.

The *Doncaster Gazette* of 22 September 1905 said that the race over a two mile course for the Cup proved a very interesting event. For the last quarter of a mile, Bachelor's Button, pictured above, had a deadly rival in Mark Time as they were neck and neck. The issue trembled in the balance, but in the last few paces Bachelor's Button vindicated the judgement of his backers by getting his head in front and keeping it there past the post. It was only a small field but the contest was the best of the day. The cup itself was a good example of British workmanship, and consisted of an antique silver centrepiece and four antique silver candlesticks.

Leading in Radium, winner of the Doncaster Gold Cup in 1908.

Amadis, winner of the Gold Cup in 1909. The *Doncaster Chronicle* of 17 September 1909 said, 'The cup was won by Lord Falmouth with the three year old Amadis, a son of Love Wisely himself the winner of an Ascot Gold Cup…The animal to give Amadis most trouble was the French candidate Rou Herode…Had not Amadis been as fit as this fellow the spoils would have gone to France…Amadis was indeed turned out in magnificent condition and in congratulating his trainer, W.M. Waugh, on his colt's victory one may add congratulations also to Waugh's employers, the Duke of Westminster, Lord Falmouth and Lord Coventry on the steps they have taken to secure a continuation of Waugh's services.'

Lemberg, winner of the Gold Cup in 1911. The *Doncaster Chronicle* of 21 September 1911 gave these incidental details, 'Doncaster Cup, value 200 sovs, with 1,100 sovs in specie in addition, out of which the second receives 200 sovs and the third 100 sovs, weight for age; penalties and allowances. Two miles and one furlong. Mr Fairie's b c Lemberg, by Celene-Galicia, 4, 10–0………F. Wooton.' The newspaper included these details of the race, 'A beautiful finish was witnessed between Lemberg and Kilbroney, and as the pair flashed past the winning post the favourite only had a neck advantage, but Wooton on the winner could have increased the margin slightly had he wished.'

Athford, winner of the Gold Cup in 1911.

PORTLAND PLATE

The Portland Handicap is a flat horse race in the United Kingdom open to thoroughbreds which are three years old or above. It is run over a distance of 5 furlongs and 140 yards at Doncaster Racecourse, and it takes place annually during the St Leger meeting in September. It is a handicap race and was first run in 1855. Americus Girl is seen here winning the race in 1909.

ST LEGER

Charles Watson Wentworth, 2nd Marquess of Rockingham (1730–82) owner of Alabaculia, seen here, first winner of the St Leger in 1776, produced a number of fine horses at his Wentworth Stud. Among the sportsmen whose names were much to the fore at Doncaster at that period was a Lt-General Anthony St Leger, who resided at Park Hill, and it was on his proposition that the race was founded. One may be quite certain that neither he nor those who were associated with him had any idea of the vast importance which was afterwards attached to the race. The St Leger was the first stake for three-year olds ever run for at Doncaster and was one of the last races run on the old course on Cantley Common, a little beyond Rose Hill Farm, and the course was one of two miles.

The St Leger Stakes is the oldest of the five British Classic Races and also the final leg of both the colts' and fillies' Triple Crowns. Between the St Leger meetings of 1789 and 1790 the weights were altered for the first time since the institution of the of the race, and it may be noted in connection with this that so far honours had been pretty evenly divided between colts and fillies. During the whole of his racing career, Hambletonian, the winner of the 1795 St Leger (seen here), was only beaten once. Altogether he won twenty-one races, these including the St Leger and the Doncaster Cup, which he won twice. Owned by Sir Charles Turner he further sired over 140 winners, whose gross winnings amounted to nearly £40,000. This depiction was painted by John Nost Sartorius Stipple and etched by John Whessel.

Although by no means a favourite at starting, Orville soon reassured his backers in this race, as he took the lead at the outset, was never headed, and won very easily. John Singleton Jnr rode Orville. The Thoroughbred Heritage website says 'Orville was a big, plain-headed racehorse of great stamina and exceptional durability, considered one of the great four-mile horses of his era.

He was a successful sire of Classic winners, and several of his sons also got one or more Classic winning colts...' John Singleton Jnr had a peculiarly short and sad career. Originally intended for the medical profession, he rejected this in favour of becoming a jockey, entering the Duke of Bedford's stables. He quickly proved himself likely to do great things in the saddle, and after some previous work for Earl Fitzwilliam, gave the latter his second St Leger in 1802. Singleton was twenty-six at that time, and the winning of the famous race proved to be his first and last great triumph – he died at Newmarket three months later 'highly respected, esteemed and lamented.'

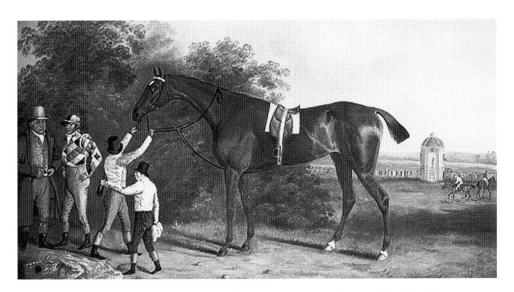

There was a falling-off in the number of subscribers and starters for the race of 1813 and there were no less than ten false starts before the seventeen runners got underway. The race formed one of the five great betting races of the year which were all won by the first favourite. When the 1813 St Leger really did get going, Tiger, Cameleopard and Hocuspocus made the running and appeared to have headed the lot until Anisidora drew to the front and won by half a head. This image was painted by Clifton Thomson (1775–1828), a Nottingham painter of animal portraits, particularly racehorses, and sporting scenes.

The betting before the 1815 St Leger was even on Filho da Puta, 5-2 and 3-1 against. Restoration made the running and maintained a lead for half a mile, when Dinmont headed him and made strong play as far as the Red House, where Filho da Puta, who had been in close attendance, had the race well in hand and won in a common canter. Filho da Puta made another appearance at Doncaster in 1816, winning a sweepstakes over the St Leger course, and afterwards winning the Gold Cup very easily. He is seen here painted by Henry Barnard Chalon (1770–1849) animal painter to the Princes of Wales and Duke and Duchess of York.

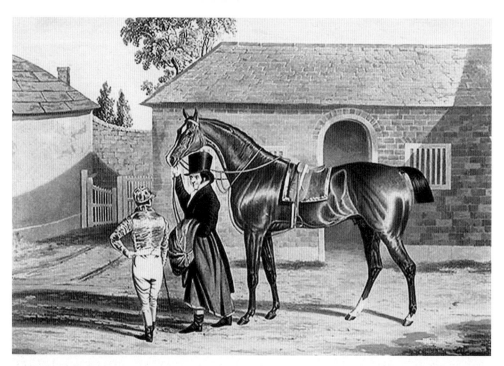

The St Leger of 1819 was run twice. The circumstances were unusual, and excited a good deal of interest at the time. A field of nineteen runners faced the starter, and of these fourteen seemed to get away without a hitch when the flag fell, but the remaining five were left behind. 'Not being ready' was the report without there being an explanation. The fourteen starters finished the course, Antonio winning, but the stewards declared a false start, and ordered the race to be run again. This time only ten horses started, Antonio not being among them and Sir Walter won. An appeal was made to the Stewards of the Jockey Club and they judged that the race should have been given to Antonio; and consequently that the stewards should not have allowed a second race. Antonio never did anything of consequence either before or after that. Antonio is painted here by J.F. Herring and engraved by Sutherland.

In the 1821 St Leger, Coronation got off with a lead, which he retained for three quarters of a mile, when Lunatic came up and went in front for nearly the same distance. Jack Spigot, Fortuna and Coronation then drew away for a fine race home, which was cleverly won by Jack Spigot by half a length. Jack Spigot was a very beautiful foal, but his dam had such galloping fits in the paddock as almost to knock the youngster to pieces, so that it was necessary to procure another mare to bring him up. It is also mentioned that Jack Spigot took such a dislike to his jockey William Scott that he would never allow him to come into his box, and showed great anger if he even heard his voice. Jack Spigot was the first of nine horses which William Scott steered to victory in the St Leger. This painting is by John Frederick Herring.

Barefoot was a chestnut colt, bred by Richard (Dicky) Watt of Bishop Burton, Yorkshire, in 1820, and won the St Leger at Doncaster in 1823. That year, twenty-seven horses went to the post and, after three false starts, twenty-three of them went away without the order to go being given. Although called back by the bugle, they ran the whole course, with Roseanne finishing first, Barefoot second and Comte d'Arthois third. It was declared a false start and in the re-run, fifteen horses had to be withdrawn, Barefoot finishing first. 'Dicky' Watt was a noted Yorkshire breeder and won the St Leger five times between 1813 and 1845.

The race of 1825 was the fiftieth since its establishment, and brought about the biggest field yet seen – no less than thirty horses facing the starter. So much interest was taken in the event, that the result was communicated to London by carrier-pigeon, and to Manchester by dogs which had been specially trained to follow a trail. The entrance money was reduced to £25 from 25 guineas, the weights were altered to colts 8st 6lb and fillies 8st 3lb and the course was shortened by 61yds becoming the familiar one of 1 mile, 6 furlongs and 132 yards. After a false start the lot got away on very even terms, Dauntless taking the lead and keeping it until the hill was passed, when Falcon came to the front. Two distances from home, Fleur-de-Lis, then running about fourth, fell, and Zirza went over her; Alderman, who was close in the rear, just managing to keep clear of them. Memnon, coming up on the outside, had no difficulty in going to the front, and won very easily by three lengths.

The race of 1826 was chiefly remarkable for the large sums of money won on Tarrare, owned by Lord Scarborough, who started at 20-1 against. The members of Lord Scarborough's household, pinning their faith on their noble master's horse, were fortunately able to net £2, with 500 among them. After a false start, in which the Duke of Leeds' colt ran for some distance, they got off well together, the same colt leading as far as the hill, where the Duke's filly came on and ran in front as far as the Red House, where Bedlamite, Tarrare, and Mulatto took up the running. Near the distance, Bedlamite challenged Tarrare boldly, but Lord Scarborough's colt was never headed from this point. Tarrare's success in the St Leger, indeed, was the only highlight of his career. A public house at Tickhill, Doncaster, part of Lord Scarbrough's estate once held the title of the Tarrare Inn, but has since closed.

The 1827 St Leger was particularly famous as a duel in the long-running battle between the North of England (here represented by Matilda) and the South (represented by Mameluke). 'A handsomer little filly than Matilda, and a finer and more slashing colt than Mameluke, never met together on any race-course' said Thomas Henry Taunton in *Portraits of Celebrated Racehorses*, vol. II, London 1887. Matilda was bred by the Hon. Edward Petre of Stapleton Park, Yorkshire. Her jockey, James Robinson, rode her without spurs, as Herring shows in the painting. Matilda's odds were 10–1, while the much larger Mameluke was the favourite at 5-2. He was unsettled by a series of fiendishly engineered false starts and eventually started at 100-30, to much muttering from the crowd, 'as the jealousy of a south-country horse winning the St Leger is too well-known to be enlarged upon,' Taunton said. Normally even-tempered, Mameluke became almost unmanageable and Chifney had great difficulty getting him to the post. Matilda shot away and was on the top of the hill before Mameluke was half-way. Mameluke staged a magnificent comeback, but Matilda won by half a length, preserving the honour of the North.

Mr Petre's third St Leger winner, the Colonel, did a good deal to make himself talked about in 1828. He was a small, short horse with very fine speed, high and fighting in his action. The Colonel won the St Leger with ease by three lengths, the winner's subsequent performances were not particularly brilliant or noteworthy. The Colonel is painted here by James Pollard and in the distance on the right, Belle Vue house may be seen.

In 1830 there was a thunderstorm of considerable violence raging as the horses went to the post, but they got away to a capital start. Emancipation took the lead, with Splendour and Maria close behind, and Priam, the Cardinal, Hassan, Moss Rose, Brunswicker, and Birmingham next in evidence. They ran in this order as far as the Red House, where Birmingham drew up to Emancipation, who kept his lead till the distance was reached, where Priam challenged him, a sharp struggle resulting in Birmingham beating Priam by half a length. J.S. Fletcher states, 'Of Birmingham's subsequent career there is little to record-his greatest accomplishment, next to having won the St Leger, appears to have lain in his trick of following [breeder] Mrs Beardsworth around her dining room table as if he had been a lap dog or a tame cat.'

In 1836 there were three false starts before the race got underway. At the Red House, John Day brought Elis, owned by Lord Lichfield, to the front, and, never being headed, won with ease by two lengths. A good deal of interest was attached to Elis' victory in the St Leger because of the presence in the race of Beeswing, whose career between 1835 and 1842 was an almost unbroken succession of triumphs.

The race of 1839 produced the first dead heat since the foundation in 1776. Charles XII (owned by Major Yarbourgh), and Euclid (owned by a Mr Thornhill) passed the post together, afterwards running the race off, with the result that Charles XII won by a head. The horses were very different in appearance. Charles XII stood 16 hands at three years old, and was of delicate constitution; Euclid, who stood 15 hands 2ins, was an animal of muscular power, good legs, and of showy looks generally. The two close finishes which they made and the way in which they left all the rest behind them in the dead heat, proved them to have been well matched and much superior to their competitors. Charles XII won the Gold Cup two days later.

Sir Tatton Sykes won the 1846 St Leger by half a length, winning £2,925. The horse, owned by William Scott, had been named after his breeder, Sir Tatton Sykes (1772–1863), though his original name was Tibthorpe. This image was published in the *Illustrated London News* on 26 September 1846, and shows sir Tatton Sykes leading in the winner.

The race of 1848 began with a bizarre incident, the field getting away from the starting post without orders, and the jockeys were each fined £5, with the exception of Marson, who had pulled up immediately and who was only fined £3. These penalties were subsequently reduced to £3 in the case of the worst offenders, and £1 in Marson's case. The winner, Surplice, bred by Lord George Bentinck and foaled in 1845, was sold as a two-year-old to Mr Mostyn, and by him resold in 1847 to Lord Clifden. It was always a source of grief to Lord George Bentinck that he had not retained possession of Surplice. As a two-year-old, Surplice met with an unusual accident – he was so frightened by a snowstorm that he attempted to clear a stone wall and turned a somersault over it, but without injury.

The 1849 race was a dead certainty, The Flying Dutchman had matters all his own way, and won easily by two lengths. Under Charles Marlow's guidance, he secured some of the largest prizes then to be won. His run in the St Leger was an easy journey. Marlow, who rode him in all his great engagements, considered that he improved as he got older, and had declared of him, when he first mounted him for a gallop, that he had 'never been on such a one before.' Closely associated with The Flying Dutchman's fame and glory, poor Marlow himself, 'honest as the day, but drunken and improvident,' ended his days in poverty and died in a workhouse.

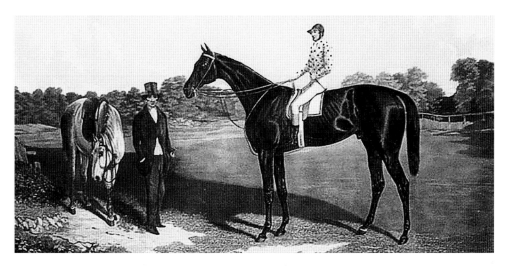

Voltigeur, after his victory in the Derby at Epsom, was a strong favourite for the 1850 St Leger, but he failed to shake off Russborough in the event, and the two passed the post together. When the dead heat was run off, the betting was 6-4 on Voltigeur, who eventually secured the verdict over the Irish-bred horse by a length only. Bred by a Mr Stephenson in 1847, Voltigeur was not a beauty to look at and his future owner, Lord Zetland, did not like his appearance as a colt, and at first would have none of him. Eventually, however, Voltigeur became Lord Zetland's property. In 1850 he beat The Flying Dutchman in the memorable race for the Doncaster Cup.

There was very little in the way of hard fighting in the 1853 race, the favourite winning easily from The Reiver by three lengths. West Australian was bred by Mr Bowes, and had a good deal of the Godolphin Arabian blood in him. He sired several well-known horses, of which The Wizard was the most famous, and was himself regarded by many judges to be the finest racehorse which the century had produced up to that day. West Australian was the first horse to win the Triple Crown in England: the Derby, St Leger, and the Ascot Gold Cup, all in 1853. This picture is from a painting by Harry Hall (1816–82) signed, inscribed and dated 1853.

In 1864, Blair Atholl, the fourth son of Stockwell to win the St Leger, was a bright, blaze-faced chestnut, standing over 16 hands high. He was bred by Mr W. I'Anson in 1861. His performances were not many but they were all great. He won the St Leger by two lengths from General Peel, and was never seen on the turf again. Sold in the Middle Park ring, he was announced by Mr Tattersall as 'the best horse in the world', and was sold to the Cobham Stud Company for 12,500 guineas. He sired several famous horses – among them Silvio, Prince Charlie, Scottish Queen, and Glenalmond – and died at Cobham in 1882. This is an oil on canvas by Harry Hall (1816–82), signed, inscribed and dated 1865.

When fairly in line for home in the 1881 St Leger, Lucy Glitters was done with, and Iroquois, shooting to the front the moment jockey Fred Archer called upon him, drew away from Geologist from the distance, and won cleverly by a length amid the most intense excitement. The value of the stakes was £5,450. Iroquois, a two-year-old, won the Chesterfield Stakes at Newmarket and the Lavant Stakes at Goodwood, and in 1881 won the Newmarket Stakes, the Derby, the Prince of Wales Stakes, the St James Palace Stakes, the St Leger and the Newmarket Derby.

One of the greatest winners that ever lived, Donovan, in 1888 and 1889 won in the stakes alone over £55,000. As a two-year-old he won the Brocklesby Stakes at Lincoln, the Portland Stakes at Leicester, the New Stakes at Ascot, the Hurstbourne Stakes at Stockbridge, the July Stakes at Newmarket, the Ham Stakes at Goodwood, and the Buckenham Stakes, the Hopeful Stakes, the Middle Park Plate, and the Dewhurst Plate at Newmarket. In 1889 he carried off the Newmarket Stakes, the Derby, the Prince of Wales Stakes, the St Leger, the Royal Stakes at Newmarket, and the Lancashire Plate at Manchester.

H.R.H the Prince of Wales's horse Persimmon won the 1896 St Leger. Before racing commenced, a few bets were traceable to this important event, but to show what was thought of the opportunity, bar Persimmon and Labrador, one well-known bookmaker at once launched out, and offered 1,000-10 against any others. No one, however, had the courage to respond to this, and the race may be said to have resolved itself from the very first, so far as the wagering went, into a competition between two. An early bet was the laying of 'five monkeys' on the Prince's colt, but after this, 900-200 was accepted that he did not win. All this time Labrador was being nibbled at 6-1 and 11-2; but when the numbers of the seven runners were hoisted, Persimmon was on the tongue of all the backers again, with the result that at flag fall the odds were lengthened to 11-2. In the final reckoning the Prince's horse was an easy winner, amid great cheering, by a length and a half. Persimmon had a particularly successful career from the very beginning and won stakes to the value of £34,726. The picture above was engraved by an anonymous artist after a painting by Isaac Cullin.

Considered such an absolute certainty for Galtee Moore, the punters simply refused to bet against the Hibernian before racing in 1897. Furthermore, they would not even make a legitimate tender bar one. Eventually one or two did accept 7-1 that the Guineas and Derby winner did not do the treble, but his followers being legion, 1,000-120 was at length betted. As expected, there were five runners, and with the elevation of their numbers longer odds were laid; indeed, the Limerick-bred colt ended up at 10-1 on. Galtee Moore won by three-quarters of a length. Without doubt the best three-year-old of 1897, Galtee Moore carried everything before him, and in this and the preceding year won around £70,000 for J. Gubbins.

Bayardo, winner of the 1909 St Leger, in which Edward VII's horse Minoru also ran and was well beaten. The *Doncaster Chronicle* of 10 September added the following details about the race, 'After parading, in the order of the card, the field reached the post a few minutes before time…A quarter of a mile from home Valens drew to the front, followed by the Story, Mirador, and Bayardo, and at the distance Bayardo challenged, and drew out clear to win very easily by a length and a half; half a length between second and third, Minoru [the king's horse] was fourth.'

The *Doncaster Gazette* of 9 September 1910 said that the St Leger 'will be one of the most memorable for the vastness of the crowd by which it was followed and for the exacting closeness of the finish…The Common on Wednesday [Leger Day] was a wonderful sight – two great masses of closely packed constantly moving humanity – separated by a band of light green turf along which the steeds were to go, carrying with them so much of human interest, of hopes and fears and material issues…the most expensive enclosures seemed almost as packed as the shilling ring…The favourite [Lemberg 6-4 on] was beaten at the distance and Swynford [6-4 against], resisting the strenuous challenge of Bronzino got the better of a thrilling finish by a head; a length and a half divided second and third.'

Prince Palatine, winner of the 1911 St Leger. The *Doncaster Chronicle* of 14 September 1911 recorded that 'during a brief delay at the post, Prince Palatine kicked Atmah,' but 'ultimately a good start was effected…' Seven furlongs from home, Prince Palatine joined Beaurepaire carrying on the running, who was beaten before entering the straight, at which juncture King William, Lycaon and Pietri speedily improved their positions. The last named, however, soon dropped away, and though Lycaon raced into second place below the distance, he could not make the slightest impression on Prince Palatine, who won, pulling up by six lengths. There were three lengths between second and third.

Polemarch, winner of the St Leger of 1921. The *Doncaster Chronicle* of 9 September 1921, under the title 'Dark Horse Wins Again', reported, 'The famous Yorkshire roar, about which we have heard so much, was merely a gasp when Polemarch flashed past first past the post on the historic St Leger course... Nearly every one met seemed to have come to the conclusion that the race was a walk over for Craig-an-Eran, and had backed it accordingly. Many, it is true, had backed Thunderer and Westward Ho... When Polemarch claimed the laurels the multitude seemed simply staggered. They could not raise a cheer, their throats were too dry, so they merely gasped, inaudibly for the most part. Here was another surprise, another dark horse. There were some lucky Doncaster people who backed it both ways, but we believe their number was limited.'

Under the heading 'Record Crowds for Return of St Leger to Town Moor,' the *Doncaster Gazette* of 12 September 1946 said that happy jostling crowds armed with raincoats and umbrellas defied 'the weatherman's predictions and flocked in their thousands to see the first St Leger on Town Moor since 1938 leaving towns and villages practically deserted. Airborne was the favourite [at 3-1] and won a magnificent victory,' said the newspaper. Airborne was a lucky winner for the Airborne Forces Security fund as the horse's owner, J.E. Ferguson, had promised that if Airborne won the St Leger he would head the list of donations to the fund. Ferguson subsequently gave 100 guineas.

A victory salute from Frankie Dettori on Santou, winner of the 220th running of the St Leger, 1996. The *Doncaster Star* of 16 September 1996 reported, 'A crowd of almost 22, 000 at Doncaster Racecourse saw one of the best finishes to the St Leger Classic for many years. A roar went up as… Frankie Dettori overhauled Dushyantor yards from the winning post. Doncaster Racecourse officials were thrilled with the attendance…which was 20 per cent up on last year's figure for Leger Day. At one stage caterers sold out of champagne but apart from the one arrest for drunkenness, police reported no trouble.'

At the 221st St Leger the storm clouds held off until after 4-4 favourite Silver Patriarch crossed the line, delighting punters. Jockey Pat Eddery notched up his 4,000th winner and became only the third rider to reach the historic landmark. The massive Doncaster crowd raised the roof as Eddery raced to victory ahead of Frankie Dettori who had hoped to ride his third Leger winner in three years. The *Doncaster Star* of 15 September 1997 added further details about the occasion, 'Wealthy suited businessmen and elegant women in designer hats sipped champagne in the members' enclosure while racing fans searched for the best odds prior to the big race. As always, extrovert tipster John McCririck drew an excited crowd and dazzled racegoers in front of the nation's television cameras. Before the start of the meeting a World War Two Spitfire circled overhead to add extra spice for the crowd.'

Acknowledgements

I would like to thank the following people for their help: David Appleyard, Colin Burley (for the loan of books and prints), Malcolm Barnsdale (for sourcing some of the old prints), Eric Braim, David Clay (Yorkshire Post Newspapers) Stuart Hastings (Sheffield Newspapers), David Kessen (*Doncaster Star*), Hugh Parkin (for patiently photographing the old prints), Mike Shepherd and Jane Smart (Sheffield Newspapers).

A special thank you is due to my son Tristram Tuffrey who trawled through many newspapers in Doncaster Reference Library for information.